To my colleagues,
past, current, and future

All the stories in this book are true, however,
I have changed the names of my colleagues,
to protect the innocent (and the not-so-innocent!).

Acknowledgments

WINSTON CHURCHILL compared writing a book to the creation of a monster, and it was true: The bigger this baby got, the more help I needed. First, heartfelt thanks to my reading team for their wisdom and guidance when my courage faltered, Cindy Cremona, Tauni G., Nancy Haller, Megan Linnemeier, and Colleen Pelton. I'm indebted to my editor, Marla Markman, for her hard work and smart suggestions. She brought great clarity to the book. And many thanks to my artist sista, Betsy Schulz, and the team at 1106 Design for making my book beautiful. My parents and siblings were kind enough to read drafts and listen to me alternately drone on or go on a rant. Much appreciation is due to my friends, neighbors, and family who put up with my permanent state of distraction this year. And as always, my deepest thanks to my husband, Tom Harvey, for making everything possible.

Contents

The Spirit of the Discreet Guide

HELLO. DURING MY CAREER, I've had the opportunity to advise and mentor many women and learned that honest, straight talk is the best way to communicate the do's and don'ts of working with men. Seven years ago, I began formally collecting material for this book when guys complained to me about my female co-workers but wouldn't say anything directly to the women. It sometimes occurred to me that the battle of the sexes had been transported into the corporate world without any open acknowledgment of it. I also observed that female senior executives and career advice books for women avoided the tough issues—those related to gender, emotions, and hostile behavior—precisely the ones I felt we needed to address. "How come we're not talking about this?" I asked myself. I broach them here "discreetly," so you and I can talk about them in private.

I don't know how you happen to be holding this book, but it is my sincere hope that it helps you. I was inspired to write it to extend a hand to ambitious women working in corporate America, in organizations that are run and predominately populated by men. This book is my way to reach women whom I haven't had the privilege of meeting, in an attempt to make their corporate experience lighter and brighter. As each of us becomes more comfortable and confident working in a man's world, we pave the way for the women who come after us. I am passionate about improving the success rates for women in corporate America, not only to increase the number of women in senior leadership roles, but to make the work life for each one a little happier. If I can help one, just one fainting sparrow, this book will be a success.

I'd love to hear your story. You can contact me at my website, discreetguide.com.

CHAPTER ONE

First Principles

THIS CHAPTER LAYS THE FOUNDATION for the book. We'll discuss the discrimination you're likely to encounter working in a man's world, how it's manifested, and how you can defend yourself so it doesn't derail you. Although it's tempting to blame men for our discomfort in the belly of the beast, that attitude won't ultimately enable your success. Many of my female colleagues dropped out as they got discouraged and felt under-appreciated. Sometimes there are good reasons to drop out, but better preparation will keep you from falling victim to the bad ones. Lastly, I encourage you to think critically about the advice in this book to ensure you get the most out of it.

The Facts of Life

After I'd been promoted to CFO, I was invited to participate in a panel discussion for a professional women's group. The topic was "How to Become a Successful Female Executive," presumably because there weren't many of them around. Our first planning teleconference started badly.

"My parents told me I could be whatever I wanted to be," one participant said spritely.

"I just don't think there really is a glass ceiling anymore," said another.

"That was more relevant before," said another.

After a few minutes of this cheerful chitchat, I broke in.

"Look," I said, "statistically, we know women earn less than men do for comparable jobs, and male CEOs radically outnumber female CEOs in large companies. We know it, and our audience knows it. So I think we can't avoid talking about it.

There was a brief silence, then one of the members sighed and said, "I know I would have been made CFO sooner if I were a man."

A partner at a national firm then spoke up:

"We've had a program for twenty years specifically designed to bring women up through the ranks and make them partner, and to this day, I am the only female partner in the local office."

"Okay," I said, "let's talk to them about *that*."

Open Eyes, Strong Shield

There's no doubt the glass ceiling exists, or whatever you want to call the real and malicious discrimination against women in the workforce. Although women have made tremendous strides in gaining influence in corporate America and in government, they're still absent from the most prestigious and powerful positions. They're paid less than men at almost every level. If they do attain a position of authority and stumble, the vitriol spewed upon them is awe-inspiring. Weren't you surprised by how much hatred and resentment was directed at Hillary Clinton despite her having "stuck by her man" and her personal level of courage and grit? What about Sarah Palin? Wow. Even Oprah seems to evoke a surprising amount of nastiness. It's easy to forget that our society is still very threatened by women who are self-confident and self-promoting—until misogyny raises its ugly head.

After you read this book, your eyes will be opened, and you will be more aware of gender discrimination. You may see that the male new hires are placed in divisions at the heart of the company while the females are sent to peripheral businesses. You may notice the junior males travel more than the females (especially those with children). Credit may be given to a male peer for one of *your* ideas. Your boss may constantly interrupt you while he listens respectfully to your male counterpart. You may encounter a secretary who's downright nasty to you for no apparent reason.

What can you do about discrimination? You can't change the world, but you can prepare yourself for these eventualities and plan your strategy for how to deal with them. Then when they occur, you won't feel slighted and upset. Whether you are a recent graduate, or are moving up through middle management, or have just entered the executive ranks, you should be aware you'll face discrimination, usually covert, but sometimes overt. The corporate world isn't fair, but it won't knock you sideways if you recognize these facts of life upfront and deal with your anger and frustration now. It's not right for you to be treated differently because you're a woman, but you will be. If you prepare yourself emotionally, you can stay strong and hopeful. This book will help you learn how to shake off those events, toughen up, dig in, redouble your efforts, and move on. It will also show you how to build a wonderful and fun career despite the challenges you face.

A Woman's Work

I encountered pay discrimination early in my career in a very specific way. I was working as a mid-level manager for a company that was otherwise quite well-run. Out of curiosity one day, I ran some payroll analysis and discovered that in every job category, *every* female was paid less than *any* male. There was no classification in which a woman made more than a man. It was as though there were two pay scales for every category. In addition, the most senior positions were held exclusively by men. I was astounded.

I hope you're not waiting for me to tell you what I did to bring this travesty to the fore, transform this company into an enlightened one, and usher in a new age of pay equality because I did nothing like that. You know what I did? I ignored it.

Realistically, what could I do? Bring it to the attention of my manager? He was a somewhat insecure man, more interested in his own career than justice. This "woman's issue" would have horrified him, and if he hadn't found a way to hide the information, he would have found a way to present it as my fault, to imply *I* was the problem, not the payroll inequity. Bring it to human resources? The director was a crotchety old guy who was widely quoted as having told his assistant she was thinking with her tits. Sue the company? That wasn't how I wanted to spend my time, and that option looked pretty likely to wreck my career. So I dropped it. But I didn't forget about it, and when the chance came to transfer to another division, I took it. Not because it was a bad company, but because the odds looked a little better someplace else.

In and Out of the Men's Room

My mother and I have a running, good-natured debate about the Women's Liberation Movement and how that went down. Her version is that a group of radical, intrepid women swooped in, wrested power from a bunch of dumb white guys when they weren't looking, and tore off, waving their bras. My view is slightly different. I think more about the gentlemen who were committed to the cause—those who fought for women's rights, who knew times had changed, and that it was fair and correct for women to become full-fledged members of society. I believe we couldn't have achieved what we did without those bright and forward-looking men.

Our different views reflect in part the evolution of opinion from one generation to the next. When war is being waged, you have to have an antagonistic view of your enemy; when the war is over, you have to learn to get along. Is the war over? You could spend a whole book arguing about whether the war is over, but what's the point? If you're participating in society as a regular person, and not as a writer or a revolutionary, you need to earn a living. That probably means working, and unless your job's in a convent or a women's prison, it probably means working with men. Of course, you could always marry a millionaire and live a life of leisure, but you'll have to read some other book to get advice about that!

Newsflash: Men Are Not the Enemy

Many books about gender discrimination treat men as the enemy and blame everything on them. A surprising number encourage competition, aggression, and even cheating, to "beat men at their own game." Good grief. I see it quite differently. Gender discrimination comes from both men and women, and at times we're all guilty of it. It's a natural mistake because of the way we've been socialized. Bias against women in the corporate world isn't the fault of the men you work with, and you can't be effective if you go around hating them. That's inappropriate when you're trying to work with your colleagues—male and female—to make your company the best it can be.

I'm hopeful time will help solve this problem. We already see that each generation that comes along is more open to the notion of women in all levels of an organization. I especially observe this in men who are old enough to have daughters going into non-traditional careers and who express their great pride in and hopes for their daughters' professional success. I've benefited from their interest in *my* career and their generous mentorship as they helped me along, hoping someone will do the same for their daughters.

Men who have become accustomed to working side-by-side with women in business school are also more aware of the contributions women can make and are capable of seeing them as business partners, instead of only as girlfriends, wives, or mothers. I've encountered some young businessmen who were remarkably emancipated and clearly embraced women as equals.

And women *are* making progress, albeit slowly. We continue to see firsts in corporations, government, and education: first female CEO at IBM, first female editor of *The New York Times*, first female warship commander, first woman to pitch batting practice in major league baseball. I think these all matter. Slowly but surely, we are becoming accustomed to seeing women in non-traditional roles, showing us what's possible, and setting an example for those who follow behind. So, things are getting better.

Alone Together

I've written this book for women—just starting out or already working—who find themselves spending more and more of their time with men and who notice more frequently they're the only woman in the meeting, the only woman on their floor of the building, the only woman in the chartered van or private plane.

You can develop a sense of isolation, or begin to feel downright peculiar, when the meeting breaks up and all the guys crowd into one restroom, and you go off on your own to use the Ladies'. It can get especially weird when you realize you're the only person using that restroom the *entire* day, and all the booths are being cleaned at night in the event you might have used one.

Much has been written about the secret stuff that goes on in the Men's room during meeting breaks, how deals are made, and important information is exchanged that women are left out of—to their detriment—and how unfortunate it is that women don't get to be part of that. Bob Mankoff published a cartoon in *The New Yorker* of a woman bursting into the Men's room to discover a hidden conference room behind the door and an all-male meeting underway. "Aha!" she declares, "Just as I suspected!"

Actually, I'd just as soon *not* be there when a bunch of guys are using the facilities. And, although I'm sure some important information has been exchanged in the Men's room at some point, I gotta believe that usually not much happens except the usual and maybe some useless reiteration of the latest sports headline. Speaking for myself, I'm just as happy to give that a pass and have a quiet moment to myself.

As I stand there alone, I often think about other women also standing quietly by themselves in front of the mirror, in other companies, reflecting maybe for the first time, that they're an extreme minority. Cheer up! There are *lots* of us—we may only see each other at conferences or in airports, but there are many female executives working across America, Europe, and Asia; everywhere there are men working, there are bound to be a few foolhardy women who have infiltrated their ranks or who have taken an unexpected turn somewhere. This is a real sisterhood—women who have moved into non-traditional roles, who are motivated and excited by their work, but who look around and realize that everyone else at the table has something they don't.

Is this a bad thing? Well, you've got something they don't, and it may be more than just a physical attribute. Now that I'm older and wiser, I realize many women naturally come by skills that assist them in working situations. As our careers develop, it's useful to acknowledge and take advantage of them. It's also fun, and you'll feel more confident looking at yourself in the Ladies' room mirror.

Tuning In and Dropping Out

Statistics tell us that few women become CEOs or chairs of boards of directors. Check out the demoralizing numbers published year after year by Catalyst, a non-profit organization that tracks the progress of women in leadership roles. Even in companies that have made a conscious and deliberate effort to recruit and promote women, they seldom make the executive or partner level. What's the problem?

I think it's a combination of factors: There's a subtle reluctance to promote women; they don't always work well with men and stagnate at middle-management levels; they eventually realize they're not advancing as quickly as they would if they were male; they find this sad and discouraging; and they drop out to do something else with their time, like raising children, consulting, or starting their own business.

My business career began in the early 1990s, twenty years after women had begun entering the workforce in serious numbers. I expected to find a few high-ranking women in the organizations I worked for, and I did—*a few*. I also expected to see more women coming along behind me as the number of female business graduates was growing, and I did. What I *didn't* expect was that as my career advanced, both women ahead of and behind me would drop out long before retirement and leave the corporate world—start their own businesses, follow different career paths, or stay home with their kids. Over the next twenty years, it was disappointing to see many talented women go off to do their own thing. The higher I rose in the organizations, the fewer women I found at my level, leaving me all too frequently the only woman in the boardroom and executive suite. Sometimes I feel like the last girl standing.

Should I Stay or Should I Go

Don't get me wrong—there are good, uplifting reasons to leave. Entrepreneurs, devoted mothers, and women who prefer an academic or non-profit organization are genuinely motivated to pursue their passions outside of the corporate world. A woman who drops out of corporate life because she discovers she hates the work has a legitimate reason to leave, and it was probably a poor career choice for her in the first place. However, I knew a number of women who offered socially-acceptable reasons for dropping out (children or self-employment), but I knew them well enough to know that those were not the real reasons. They all had a different story about what happened, but a common theme was that they ultimately felt under-appreciated and ran out of steam. I talk to too many women who left the corporate world, *not* because they didn't like the work, but because they felt they were sidelined, stagnating, or over-stressed. They may have had some bad experiences with their managers or gotten crossways in office politics. They're often pretty bitter about how things ended, and that's a real shame.

Well, now that we're all thoroughly depressed, what can we do about this? Is leaving corporate America always the best option for disenchanted executive women? What if the dropouts had been provided with better tools for the workplace, particularly for getting along with men? Before another one leaves and abandons me in the Ladies' room, I want to share with you what I've learned about working with men and my suggestions for how to do it well. Even after the dozens of advice books that have been written for women in the workplace, apparently we haven't said the right things because women are still dropping out in droves. Men aren't dropping out. They're staying. Somehow they're more comfortable with the corporate world than women are. Many factors are in play here, but I believe a critical issue is that women don't know how to thrive in a male-dominated environment.

Hold It Right There, Lady

Throughout my career, I've noticed that women don't always behave in their own self-interest and sometimes seem unaware of how men "see" them. Employees must shine in the eyes of their superiors, who are usually men. It makes me sad to see an ambitious young woman damage her reputation and lose her upward mobility because she misinterprets important signals or feedback from men or behaves in ways that are alarming and make them uncomfortable. We'll look at lots of these in this book.

You You You

If you grew up around guys, played sports with guys, or had a lot of guy friends, count yourself lucky. All that experience will be very applicable, even in the corporate world. If you're more of a feminine girl and mostly hang out with other women, you may have to read this book more closely. It's hard to change your behavior, especially patterns you've developed over a lifetime. But, if you're aware of some of the pitfalls in a corporation, you're halfway to avoiding them.

By arming yourself with advice in this book, you're more likely to succeed in companies primarily run and populated by men. By working to your highest level, you'll achieve greater job satisfaction and may stay longer at your corporation. But you must work collaboratively with men and avoid the mistakes that have brought down other ambitious female executives. You'll have to be honest about your level of commitment and how willing you are to adopt new styles and behaviors to get along in the corporate world. As you rise through the ranks, each level will require more and deeper skills that you must develop if you don't inherently possess them. You'll have to work hard, but developing yourself can bring much joy.

If you're lucky, you'll find some skills come easily to you, more so than to men, *because* you're a woman. You're likely to have excellent coping skills, better powers of observation, and greater emotional intelligence than your male peers. Those attributes will serve you mightily during the course of your career. Through your wits and goodwill, you can help educate your colleagues about how a great female leader looks and acts.

So what if the statistics are against you? You've probably bucked the trend in all kinds of ways already to get where you are. Who knows? Maybe the stars will align perfectly, your remarkable talents will be recognized by those who count, and you'll become CEO in record time! You can also be very proud of all your accomplishments because everything you achieve is in spite of the odds being slightly stacked against you. Remember that if you're not made CEO, it may not be your fault. You may be working as hard as you can and doing everything right, but there's an undercurrent of prejudice that forces you to persevere and prove yourself over and over. But you like a challenge, right? What's the alternative: Sit on the couch and sulk? That'd be lame.

We all have characteristics that help or hinder us in our career. Maybe you have a strange laugh or unruly hair. Maybe you have naturally good social skills or a sunny personality. We have to work with what we have, and being a woman is just one part of your potential. As I told my audience from the beginning of the chapter, "You can't change your gender, or it would be kind of *extreme* to do so. I'd hope there was a very good reason for it—not just that it's better for your career!"

Time to Grow

In general, the corporate world is organized and run in ways that have benefited companies for decades, if not hundreds of years. Management theories come and go, but some fundamentals remain because we've found good business practices make companies efficient, productive and profitable. If you expect your corporation to accommodate you, embrace you and mold itself around you, despite your bad habits and idiosyncrasies, you probably won't be as successful as you would like.

People often use game analogies to talk about the workplace, and I do, too (playing the game, the playing field, winning), but let me remind you: Business is serious; it is not a game. If your superiors don't think you can contribute more at the next level, they won't promote you. They can't afford to, no matter how much they like you. Their responsibility is to move up individuals who will make the company stronger. You must exhibit the qualities they need at that level or show that you can acquire the appropriate skills. Good business people, both men and women, are deadly serious about this. It's not personal; they're not being mean. It's their job.

You'll have to seek out and embrace feedback—even negative feedback. You may be told your behavior is unacceptable or ineffective. You may get a confusing comment on your personnel evaluation. You may receive some oblique feedback with a hint of something wrong, but you're not sure what. You may *not* be told anything, which is worse, but you eventually figure out there's something holding you back. To succeed in the corporate world, you'll have to work on something—all of us do—to become the extraordinarily skilled and well-rounded executive who can handle those big jobs.

If you've had teachers, parents, or coaches who were pretty direct and didn't beat around the bush when they told you what you were doing wrong, you probably understand how to take feedback unemotionally and act on it. Other women might not have been as lucky—people have treated them gently because they didn't want to hurt their feelings. Fortunately, good training is available for how to actively give and receive feedback. In addition, many women are naturally open to self-analysis and self-improvement. They can absorb feedback and put it into action more quickly than their male peers.

When you get feedback, embrace it, and thank the person who gave it to you. You've been given a gift and one all too rare from typical, mediocre managers. And then—here comes the hard part—put it in action. You'll have to move out of your comfort zone and modify a piece of yourself: your behavior, attitude, approach, natural inclinations—something. If you're not willing to change, you can't be successful in the corporate world.

Doesn't that sound harsh? I think I'm scaring *myself.* Actually, change can be fun, and learning more about yourself and how you come across to people is eye-opening. Knowing you're getting better at your job as you move up the career ladder is inspiring, and that helps you help others around you. Having faith in the feedback loop will keep you from getting defensive when someone is critical of you. You need that feedback, and it's a brave person who gives it to you. Demonstrate your willingness to accept criticism, and show you can handle it. The bottom line is, you'll have to change—think of it as growing, which is a happy word.

Skeptical Spectacles and a Critical-Thinking Cap

Formal financial reports begin with a Safe Harbor statement the lawyers make us put in. It basically says that everything in the report could very well be hogwash. So, here's my Safe Harbor statement: Not everything in this book may be right for you. If something I've written sounds ridiculous, don't do it! If it makes sense, try it out. The business world is too full of mindless conformity. Don't let that be you. Put on your skeptical spectacles and your critical-thinking cap, and you may discover your work life just got a whole lot easier because you can see what's really important and what's just silly.

I've had the good fortune to get along with men most of my life. It probably helps I had two dads, one older brother, one husband, and two sons. Sometimes, too, it's easier to see what someone else is doing wrong than to be objective about your own behavior. I'm pretty unemotional and observant which helped me figure out a few things early in my career. Nevertheless, I'm far from perfect, and some incidents I look back on just make me cringe. So, in some cases, you'll have to do as I say instead of as I did!

Finally, be aware that the corporate world is a rarified and strange environment, structured by a formal hierarchy and artificial relationships. Behaviors that are appropriate in corporations, or even necessary for survival, are not the same as those that you are comfortable with in real life. I would hesitate to transfer my advice in this book to your personal life—there may be occasions when it is appropriate, but I suspect the best motto is: Don't try this at home.

You Talkin' to Me?

Throughout my career, I've hated it when men made sexist remarks about women. "Women can't get along." "Women never notice what kind of plane they're flying in." "Women can't read maps." It bugged me because there's so much variability among women that there are always exceptions to these generalizations. Not to mention that they were often demeaning. For heaven's sakes, some women are *pilots*—you think they don't notice what kind of plane they're flying? It also used to irk me when women would make sexist remarks about men. "Men can't multi-task." "All they think about is sex." "Men are babies when it comes to pain." Ah, hang on a sec. You think men can't handle pain? I can think of a few exceptions, and I'll bet you can, too. I don't like this trash-talking about the opposite sex, and I think these stereotypes are inaccurate and misleading. So, why am I doing it all over the place in my own book?

When we're discussing gender issues in the workplace, it's helpful to use generalizations. Obviously, you know that not all guys act alike, and they can't be classified in categories. Each one is unique and special. Please don't interpret my general observations as denigrating, as though I mean to deny each man his individuality. I use generalizations, however, because I've observed similar patterns of behavior from men and women that sometimes work against each other. It's painful to watch a woman behave in ways that negatively affect how she comes across to a guy. It's disappointing to hear men criticize a female colleague when I suspect she doesn't realize what she's doing wrong. But I can't talk about these issues without using generalizations.

Beware, human beings are far more complicated than I present them here; your situation will be different which means you'll have to apply my advice delicately and be smart about whether or not it's appropriate. You must critically assess whether the issues I identify in this book are relevant to you or not. I don't mean to imply that you're a nitwit and that you're going to behave like all these dumb women in my book. You have your own strengths and weaknesses, natural abilities, and areas you need to focus on. You're not exactly like me or the other women in this book, which means your path will be unique—that's why it will be so interesting.

CHAPTER TWO

Your Sistas and You

IN DEFIANCE OF THE STEREOTYPES we just mentioned, this chapter is about you and what makes you unique. This is an opportunity to think about your individual values, what makes you different from everyone else, and how you will preserve and protect yourself. We will also discuss what being different means to men and how that perspective can give you some insights into their mentality. Executives are sometimes overly preoccupied with appearances—this chapter encourages you to focus on behaviors, rather than clothes and makeup. Finally, as part of the corporate team, you can subvert typical misogyny by consciously supporting your female co-workers, and some examples are given for how to do so.

Whose Girl Are You?

Although you'll want to change and grow, one thing you must preserve is *who* you are. Because the playing field is slightly tilted against you (not impossibly so—just a little bit), you must define your own terms of success and establish your own metrics to measure yourself by. You may not be able to compare yourself to your male peers or with where you expected to be at a certain stage of your career—it's too hard to forecast how all the contributing factors will intersect. But you must be true to yourself, take a clear-eyed view of your own qualities, consider what really matters to you, and determine how much you're willing to commit to your career. These are highly personal assessments and choices. Don't let someone else's view of what you should be govern your own.

These priorities will clarify your ideal balance between your personal life and work life. Be honest about how your personal priorities fit into the needs of your organization and recognize you'll probably be more career-oriented at some stages than others. You may be highly motivated at the beginning of your career, but a time may come when you have to back off because of pressing personal issues. That's okay. It's natural to experience ups and downs, and these cycles shouldn't upset you as long as you maintain a long-term view of your career. Stick with your plan, be patient, and don't get discouraged. There will be rough patches, but don't be too hard on yourself.

Take It Slow

Don't try to rush your career. You can't become experienced in your job in a few months; it takes time to build skills and practice them at each level. Aim to stay in each position for about two years: one year to learn it and one year to become proficient in it. Make career decisions carefully and think through the impact of each one on your resumé. It takes decades to build a solid career, but it's one of life's most-rewarding endeavors.

When employees lack the experience to be successful at a particular level, but are catapulted up through the organization anyway by well-meaning but foolish managers, it results in their loss, not gain. I see this happen more frequently to men but also to very ambitious women. Ultimately, it's damaging (and stressful) to the employees because their failure usually results in termination or the elimination of their position. These employees often leave with inappropriately high salary and title expectations for their next position. They end up having to take a step down to get back into a company, and that hurts their resumés and their egos.

Let's Play

Imagine you're playing a video game called *How to Launch Your Career in Business*. As you start your mission, just out of school, you're propelled into space with some tools and resources you acquired during your education and previous work experience. You're alone in your spacecraft, and only you can navigate your ship. As you advance, obstacles are hurtling your way, other ships try to shoot you down, and you make lots of friends and a few enemies. The whole adventure is great fun, but you can't just cruise. If you don't consciously manage your flight, your spacecraft will drift aimlessly and make only random progress. However, if you stay focused, as you progress in the game, you can be elected for special missions where you learn new skills that can be added to your tool belt. These skills allow you to take on tougher and more interesting assignments to challenge you and, in turn, provide you with new and rich experiences.

This analogy for actively managing your development and enhancing your skill set is a useful way of thinking about your career. Good decision-making along the way is crucial to developing a coherent and impressive resumé. Each time you change jobs or accept a new position, ask yourself, "Will this significantly enhance my resumé? What skills will I gain that will make me better prepared for my next assignment?" Ask senior professionals in your field to look at your resumé and point out holes you should fill in order to advance. Remember a solid resumé requires lateral moves now and then; you may want to accept some positions that are broadening, rather than attempting to go straight up through an organization. Lateral moves allow you to gain an understanding of other functions and industries, overseas divisions, etc. It's easier to build a breadth of skills earlier in your career when jobs are more plentiful and your salary requirements aren't as high.

Ideally, in the early years, your resumé should reflect a logical progression of increasing responsibility, with no breaks, and some lateral moves to broaden your skills. Throughout your career, every time you change jobs, you'll be asked to explain why you left one company and joined the next. Make sure your reasons are rational. Don't fly off the handle and quit in a huff. Don't burn bridges. Make sure you leave a company on as positive a note as you can. Always take the high road when talking about former companies to your new potential employer. Your resumé is your professional report card, so make sure it's an A+. Many times, I've looked at a candidate's resumé full of short stints here and there, a jumble of titles, layoffs, and pauses, and thought, "You poor thing." Was he just unlucky, or did he make poor choices? Ultimately, even being unlucky reflects on you. Be careful.

My video game analogy is appropriate for managing your career, but not for how you'll behave inside an organization. As part of a team, you'll spend most of your efforts working toward the common good, while the resumé-enhancing aspects of your job are ancillary. When you're building your career, you're working for yourself, and you're truly on your own. No one inside your organization can tell you what the best choices are for you. Nor can anyone outside your organization clearly see what will make you happy in the long run. You alone are responsible for your success. You will and should get broad guidance as you make choices, but ultimately what you construct is of your own making. That's why you can be so proud of your progress along the way. This is all you.

You Don't Have to Cheat

Returning to our video game, how do you keep your head as obstacles and alien forces are hurtling at you? You need to know yourself, not just what your desires and strengths are, but what you're made of, what your core set of beliefs is. And, without being overly dramatic, I suggest you write them down. What does honor mean to you? Integrity? How are you going to carry yourself through your business career so that, at the end, you can hold your head up and say, "Through it all, I stayed true to my own moral core, I maintained a high ethical standard in everything I did, and I set an example for how business can be conducted with integrity." I hope your list includes items, such as telling the truth, treating employees with respect, dealing fairly with vendors, acknowledging mistakes, apologizing when you should, being clear about right and wrong, obeying the law, paying what's promised, negotiating in good faith... Moral principles can be demonstrated in the business world in many ways (and there are too many ways in which they can be undone), but it's important that you describe a set of behaviors that define *your* moral base and put a rod of steel through it that you can hold onto through thick and thin.

You'll encounter people who don't follow these principles, who lie, misrepresent results, manipulate and double-deal, and who may try to sway you or influence you to behave unethically, either subtly or openly. If you define your core values at an early stage, you'll be able to quickly identify actions that betray them, and you won't wobble under pressure. You don't have to cheat to be successful in business, and you don't want to fall into a trap someone has laid for you, assuming you're naïve. Your business identity is closely tied to your integrity and understanding of right and wrong. Don't let anyone try to change *who* you are.

Be your own girl.

Taking Care

Get ready. Now I'm going to sound like your mom. I think eating well and getting lots of exercise can really help your career. On one hand, I hesitate to bring this up because you've been told the importance of good nutrition and exercise for your health before, and you're either doing it or you're not. On the other hand, working professionals forget how physically demanding their jobs are and how they need to stay well-nourished and in good shape, simply to deal with the stresses of their job, day after day, and keep their brain working well. So, here goes.

Consider Your Choices

Your brain is your most important tool in the corporate environment. Like the rest of your body, it works best when you're hydrated, nourished, and full of energy from staying in shape. You can't expect your poor old brain to work particularly well when you get up late, rush off with no breakfast, eat some junk for lunch, drink sugary, caffeinated drinks all day, and have a super-fattening dinner late after driving home exhausted, only to get up the next day and do it again. Not only does that sound horrible, but you won't perform well, especially if you keep it up week after week.

Get up a tiny bit earlier (fifteen minutes can make a big difference), and while you're eating a piece of fruit, plan your nutrition and hydration for the day. Quick, healthful foods are available now in convenient packaging: nutrition bars, juices, trail mixes, dried fruit, soups, smoothies… It won't take much time out of your day to get your calories in at lunchtime and move right into the afternoon. Take a breather at lunchtime. Your brain needs a minute to regroup—and you're not chained to your chair—so get up and stretch or take a quick walk around the building.

I Love Oranges

They're the perfect executive food. They come in their own package, they don't need to be refrigerated, they're delicious and packed with energy, and they make your office smell nice. And, after you eat one, you have to go wash your hands, which gives you an opportunity to say hi to your staff. How cool is that? I used to peel and eat mine in the kitchen every day wherever I worked so that I could talk to the employees. It became my trademark. "We could tell you were in already," my staff would say slyly, "...by the smell. Hee hee."

Work Out for Work

How are you going to fit in your workout? Figure out how to get this into your daily routine so it becomes something you don't even think about—you just do it. Can you get a run in before you leave for work? Can you spend some time on the treadmill at lunchtime? Can you stop by the gym on the way home? Include activities as part of your workout that you enjoy and that you would miss if you *didn't* do it, whether it's listening to music or podcasts, watching TV, or chatting with a friend. This will provide an incentive when you don't feel like working out.

The benefits to regular strenuous exercise are remarkable, and it's shameful how few working women realize this. You'll feel good, both after your workout and all during the day. Your mood will be brighter. You'll look better and be proud of your muscles and sleek lines. You'll be more relaxed and have a more philosophical attitude about your job. You'll sleep well and will easily stay hydrated because you're thirsty. You'll feel calmer and better able to handle your emotions.

When life gets stressful, you need to work out. If you're upset, work out. Scary presentation coming up? Work out. Board meeting?

Work out. It really is a great problem-solver. As I got further along in my career, I finally conceded it was more important for me to get in my workout than to do some last-minute cramming for an upcoming meeting. I was fresher, more clear-minded, better able to handle decisions, questions, and difficult conversations post-workout than I would have been post-cramming. Working out before a presentation left me calmer, better able to connect to my audience, and really enjoy the experience. Try to get in as much exercise as your schedule allows. When all else fails, at least stretch for ten minutes. Then you're less likely to fall victim to the stiff necks and backaches that plague the desk-bound.

The Executive Athlete

Think of your work as though you're an athlete. You have to stay mentally flexible and strong all day long. You're multi-tasking every minute. You're trying to get your projects done, in between meetings, while the phone is ringing, your schedule is changing, and your staff is circling. There's lots to keep track of, and you want to feel on top of your game every minute. You can't suddenly be undone by a moment of low blood sugar. You really want to go-go-go and make this a productive and stimulating day. You can't do that if you have low energy and feel morose.

Now consider how long you have to keep up this pace: not just weeks or months, but *years* with relatively few breaks. You have to pamper and tend to your body very well so it can keep functioning at this level for decades. Try to establish good habits early on, and they'll pay off in a long and healthy career.

Do take the time to take care of yourself. It might just be the most important thing you do, not just for your career, but for your life. Now, don't I sound just like your mom?

You're Different and That's Only Mostly Bad

I had a conversation early in my career with a male manager who declared it could be an advantage to be a woman when building a business career. I didn't challenge him, but I was pretty skeptical. First, it had a smarmy innuendo behind it, like "You'll probably get promoted [instead of me] just because you're a darn woman." Second, that hadn't been my experience, and third, it flew in the face of all statistical evidence (and still does). I knew he was wrong, but I just thought to myself, "You don't know the half of it."

More than twenty years later, I can say, "You know what? He really didn't know the half of it." Because in some ways, he was right! Not in any way he would have understood at the time, but in a multitude of ways I've discovered since then.

Nothing Like You

Let's start with some basics. As you grow up, you discover not everyone is like you (I hope this is not a revelation). People react to this in different ways. Some people are alarmed by it, and try to make everyone like themselves, either through indoctrination or force. Others are more mellow; they accept the differences, but they're not happy about it. This tends to be the women's approach—"I know we're different in some respects, but look at all the ways we're the same!" They want to downplay the differences so we can all just get along.

Most American guys have another approach—they don't mind being different. In fact, they talk about how different (and special) they are all the time. As long as you're not *too* different, it's a positive thing. Maybe they have a unique philosophy on life, maybe they were exceptionally good at basketball, or maybe they have a weird scar they want to show you. They revel in that individuality, and they don't really understand why you're bothered about the differences.

I sometimes hear these two views played out in a conversation between a man and a woman. The guy may spend most of the conversation emphasizing how different and unusual he is, while the woman tends to verbally chase after him, explaining how she *too* feels that way, and how she had a brother who played basketball *too,* and so on. Sometimes it even builds some tension, as the man, unhappy with her attempt to match his every tale and topic, tries to pull away by driving the conversation more forcefully. She, on the other hand, may be concerned that she's failing to bond with him if she feels him slipping away. If you find yourself in such a conversation, remind yourself that the guy isn't usually looking for bonding—he just wants you to acknowledge that he's unique.

And you, girlfriend, are different. No matter how much you try to emphasize your similarities and talk about how much you have in common, you're different. One of you is male, and one is female. And guess what? The guy is acutely aware of this. He may not mention it, or he may subtly refer to it, but every moment he's with you, he's intensely aware of your femaleness. He notices it in every little thing about you—your voice, your hands, your hair, even how you smell. There's just no getting around it: You're different.

Now you can understand why guys are perplexed if a woman acts like a man. "Why does she dress like that?" they ask when a woman dresses like a man. "Does she really have to talk that way?" they wonder when a woman curses. Guys don't mind if you show a little spunk, but they don't find swearing attractive in a woman, particularly in the workplace. They don't understand why women think being different is a liability. In their minds, it's a good thing.

Da** It, They're Swearing Again

Here's a side note about swearing and bad language. Sometimes hostile guys try to isolate you with bad language to emphasize you're outside the guy group. When they swear, they'll say, "Oh, sorry, Jennifer," as though you have some kind of lock on clean language. I'd let this go once, but if they keep it up, I'd call them on it. You need to let him and the other guys in the room know you're not a prima donna, and just like lots of guys who don't swear at work, you don't, either. Sometimes looking completely mystified will get a laugh out of the other guys in the room which, in my experience, stops this behavior cold. Alternatively, you could say mildly, "I've heard that word before." You don't need to act like a guy to get along with guys, but don't let some dork make you feel like an outsider.

How Am I Different

We better talk about restrooms again. You see, unlike me, a guy wouldn't really mind being in the bathroom by himself. Guys don't go off to the bathroom together unless they have business to transact. Women, on the other hand, love to go to the bathroom together. They think it's more friendly and gives them a chance to emphasize their togetherness and solidarity.

In my casual observation, a guy doesn't usually mind being the only male in a group of females. As long as it's not a "girl's" activity that threatens his masculinity, he's into it. He might even enjoy having a temporary harem. A woman, on the other hand, may be alarmed to be the only female in a group of men if she's not accustomed to it. She may not like being "alone" and different. She may respond by trying to be "one of the guys" (imagine how *that* goes over with the guys), drinking beer, and being loud.

Keep these two perspectives in mind as you observe men and women in the workplace. It might explain strange comments like the one my manager made to me about the advantage of being a woman; it might also help you "hear" a conversation in which a man is trying to distinguish himself from you, and you might be better able to differentiate between men who treat you like you're special, in a good way, and those who treat you like a displaced person, in order to ostracize you.

Let's get back to some specifics about you.

Impressions and The Real Thing

I promise, this book will not carry on about your appearance. This topic has been covered in depth by other books; there are even some books that *only* talk about this issue. Honestly, I don't think your appearance is as important as other factors: the quality of your work, your attitude, your ability to work with people, particularly men. Plus, isn't that just like a bunch of girls to think your success depends on what you wear and how you fix your hair? If only we had as many books about How to Use Your Brain in Business as there are about What to Wear.

I will make just one suggestion: Pick a style and stick with it. There's more leeway to create your own style than the old-fashioned "dress for success" rules, but I'd avoid clothes that emphasize or show off your body (now who's being old-fashioned?). When you're working with men, those styles are very distracting. You're trying to get some work done after all! Don't constantly change your style, either. Guys are very aware of what you look like, and a change in your appearance is more disconcerting and disturbing for them than for your female co-workers. Once, when I broke my own rule and cut off nearly all my hair, my boss said sadly, "It's like having to get used to a whole new person."

Women, on the other hand, are fantastically absorbed with appearances—clothes, hair, jewelry, earrings, makeup, nails, eyebrows, scarves, shoes, bags, luggage... It's truly stunning to see how much ink is devoted to giving advice about the intricate details of women's dress at work. So, the good news is: Men don't care that much about what you wear. Yay, it's great to work with men! The bad news is your female colleagues will be much more preoccupied with your appearance.

Your Mirror

Do get a sense for the overall impression you make. Are you tall and big-boned? You may have to tone down your voice and manner so you're not perceived as over-bearing. On the other hand, you may be more like me. Early in my career, I was on a videoconference with two of my male colleagues. I was astonished to see how I looked sitting between them on the screen: I was TINY. It looked as though they'd brought their first-grader to the meeting. I realized I'd have to be "bigger" in my manner before anyone would pay attention to me. I worked on moving around and taking up more space to compensate for my small stature.

Ask your friends to tell you what part they'd give you in a movie. That will give you some insights into how you come across, the language you use, the general impression you make. Videotape yourself making a presentation. Watch yourself in the mirror to see what facial expressions you have a tendency to make and see if they're unattractive or peculiar. Record yourself to listen for verbal tics, such as saying "um" and "you know." These are all good ways to see yourself as others see you. You can adjust accordingly by practicing behaviors you feel are more representative of the real you.

Let's See Action

Focus on actions, rather than appearances. Be self-observant and self-critical. That way, you'll develop and stick with a style you're comfortable with, but you'll constantly be working on improving and controlling your behaviors. And I mean important behaviors here—how you handle an employee confrontation, dealing with the aftermath of a business crisis, working on a company-wide initiative.

I chuckle when I read the typical advice given to women: Don't smile, don't be nice, and don't ever apologize. It's mindless and superficial. Successful women come in all styles; some smile a lot and do just fine. A few executive women have even been known to apologize! So don't be silly. Focus on what's important.

I'm sometimes surprised to hear women make casual nitwit comments that can create a negative impression. For example, I once heard a young financial manager announce in the hallway that she never balanced her checkbook—she just always left enough money in her account to cover anything she might have forgotten. Excuse me? You're a *financial* manager? If you don't balance your checkbook, don't announce it. That's the kind of disclosure that will get the guys exchanging grins across the room. Don't brag about your shortcomings. Guys don't do this—for a reason. Don't say you're not good with numbers, or you'd be lost without your GPS, or you're hopeless with technology. Those are not things to be proud of.

Especially don't say you're not good with numbers. Numbers are your friends. They reveal all. Get down with them.

On the other hand, don't confuse these superficial considerations with what's profoundly important to your success—your work. I notice women aren't always objective about the quality of their work; they may not recognize when their work isn't as substantial as it should be or when they genuinely haven't worked as hard as someone else. Be honest about the balance between your personal life and your work. If you're giving more time to your personal life than your male peers are, you'll probably not advance as quickly as they will. That's how the business world works, and it makes sense that it works that way. There's nothing wrong with spending more time on your personal life, but increased job responsibilities will flow to those who seem most capable of handing them. If you have to leave at 3:30 several days a week, if you want to work from home one day a week, if you can't travel—these will limit your advancement. You must recognize that your superiors will consider these issues objectively when they need someone to work at the next level up.

Sistas

Don't underestimate the misogyny you'll encounter, particularly as you start to gain power and influence. Many people, men and women, don't like to see women in powerful roles, and they'll retaliate. You may discover that someone has been saying unkind things about you, an assistant has told an outright lie about your motivations, or you've been characterized as a bitch, a climber, a battle-axe. If so, be careful before you react; it may not even be about you. The people behind the rumors may simply be threatened by the image of a woman in charge. They're not used to it; they don't understand it; and for many people, they don't like what they don't understand. It disturbs their world view because they've been indoctrinated their entire lives about how women should behave. You're not going to change their minds easily. Their feelings run too deep and are too strong. Look at the level of hatred directed at powerful, visible women—it's not even rational. Nevertheless, there are strategies you can use to undermine this hurtful language, and they're worth pursuing. Maybe over time, we can overcome this prejudice, and misogyny will fade away into the past.

Who's Got Your Back?

Be ready. Know that with each promotion, you're at a greater risk of being attacked. As your career progresses, you must become more sensitive to the negative stereotypes of women in authority and work as hard as you can to counteract them. Deliberately cultivate a style that's defiantly *unlike* the stereotype: Be consistently friendly, warm, cheerful and humble. Take time to converse; show interest in others; be aware at all times you're fighting to shake up someone's preconceived notion of what you'll be like. And it *is* a fight, but since you come into the battle knowing what weapons your enemies will use, you have a huge advantage. Make sure that those who know you can defend you against the mindless meanies who make up lies. Over time, your record will stand up to scrutiny, and you'll have more supporters than detractors.

Be a Sista

Don't let that small-minded misogynist be you. Even if you have reservations about another woman, don't denigrate her. Support the women around you. Don't make snide remarks about women in power. Don't make fun of women on television or be catty about female politicians. It only perpetuates the misogyny and secretly gives people (especially men) a thrill when women are nasty about other women.

Watch out for your sistas after hours too. If a female colleague is getting harassed, drinking too much, or acting inappropriately, intervene and help her out. Don't let her make a mistake she'll regret forever. Often, the guys will step in also. They don't want to see a woman they like and respect be humiliated.

Be especially kind to administrative assistants: They have very hard jobs, they're paid less than you, and they face the same adversity that you do—be a sista to them. Try to make their jobs easier. Offer to help. Don't gossip about them. Don't say mean things about them behind their backs.

As you get to higher levels, it becomes harder to find out what's going on with employees, what the morale really is, and what the rumor mill is saying. People will begin withholding information from you because they're worried about retaliation or getting into trouble. See if you can cultivate some sistas lower down in the organization, who trust you enough to tell you what's really happening. They can be your eyes and ears and help you stay in touch with your organization.

Be openly supportive of your sista peers. Don't put them down to build yourself up. They're your sisters, and when one of you succeeds, you all do. Build rapport. Stop by. Be accessible. Build a reputation as a professional colleague they can rely on and trust. If one gets promoted, be *delighted*.

Express your admiration of women above you in the organization. Even if you're surprised they got to where they are, keep those thoughts to yourself. To be successful, they have demonstrated some positive qualities. If you aspire to their position, you better figure out what those are. Also, remember it's lonely for them as they rise in the organization, and the other women fall away or drop out.

Be a mentor and protector. Extend a hand to women below you in the organization. Even if it's as subtle as a smile or thumbs up, let her know you have your eye on her. That may be tremendously meaningful to her. Is she being bypassed? Scared? Bored? Intimidated? Try to see through her eyes so you can be responsive when she needs a little support. All of us have a role to play in helping the women who are coming after us by making the corporate world a bit easier for them than it was for us.

Up with You

This chapter has focused on your individuality. Now you know who you are, how to take care of yourself, what you're like, and how you're different. You know that behaviors are more important than appearances, and you've thought about how to put feedback into action. You recognize that progressing in an organization will require personal development. Each promotion will put you at increased risk of being criticized, but you know it's not personal. You're building a network of supporters who will protect you, and you are contributing to the community of sistas to help all women in your company and beyond. With that self-knowledge and support, let's venture out into the business world.

CHAPTER THREE
Early Maneuvers

THIS CHAPTER FOCUSES ON some areas that young businesswomen sometimes avoid in the early days of their career. The business world can be a scary place when you first start out, and it's a challenge to act as though you're at ease when you're not. Believe me, I know it's easier to keep a lower profile than to risk exposure and embarrassment. However, the sooner you start engaging and practicing behaviors that are hard for you, the more confident you'll feel, and eventually, the easier they'll become.

The first section is for the student approaching graduation, where we look at improving your visibility through networking and interviewing. The second section covers considerations when choosing your first company to ensure that you find an environment in which you can flourish. And the third section addresses issues you are likely to encounter in your first job, from dealing with junior male employees and office politics to gracefully moving to a new firm. We discuss the challenges of being a woman in all these situations where you are surrounded primarily by men.

School Days

Business school felt like a man's world when I went through, and given the male/female enrollment statistics, I doubt it's changed much. Women weren't as visible or as vocal as the men, and they sometimes inadvertently gave the impression they weren't as serious as the guys. Here are some suggestions to increase your visibility by asking questions, networking, and interviewing.

Making Connections

I noticed that female students too often stayed away from corporate presentations when companies came to visit the schools, so the ratio of females to males got even worse at the evening events than it was during class. I heard various lame excuses: "I have to study," "I heard that's a bad company," "I won't know anyone there." Even if they're true, you should still go. You need exposure to the business world at this stage, and those events are a great way to get it. Seeing how the executives express themselves, what their presentations look like, what questions they get excited about—this is more educational than your course material for building a great career. Here's an opportunity to become an active participant: Get engaged, ask questions, and talk to the presenters after they speak.

A word of caution here: Don't ask show-offish questions designed only to show how smart you are. Men occasionally make this mistake—and it's embarrassing how transparent it is—so, don't follow their lead. Instead, ask honest questions—ones you're genuinely interested in; the simpler they are, the better. Often, the most revealing answers come from the simplest questions. Feel free to ask your questions after the presentation if you didn't get called on in the general session. The speaker will appreciate your interest in the company and may ask your name and remember you. The presenters are frequently high-level executives surveying the room for talent. The interviewers are more likely to be lower-level managers; don't miss an opportunity to make a connection at a senior level.

I had just this experience with a company that came to my school to recruit. I hadn't heard of the company before, but it sounded interesting, so I attended the evening presentation. I was surprised to hear about their extensive international business and went up afterward to ask a few questions. Weeks later, when I walked into that executive's office, and he said, smiling, "I remember *you*," I realized my having been whisked through the interview process and invited up for a company visit was no coincidence.

Interacting with Men Is the Key to Business

Let's revisit one of the excuses our shy sister offered for not attending company presentations: "I won't know anyone there." Many young businesswomen struggle with networking, but it's extremely important. You'll have to get over your shyness, and the best way to do that is to: practice, practice, practice. I know it's intimidating to enter a room full of talking people, usually *male*, who all appear to be having the time of their lives and leaving no room in their conversation for little old you. That's why you should start working on your networking skills when you're in school, and company presentations are excellent places to do that. These skills will serve you for your entire career, so no matter how extroverted or introverted you are, it's critical to develop them. Here are a few tips for how to break into a group and meet some new people.

First, start with a good attitude. Once you get the hang of networking, it's fun. You'll meet some people, probably learn something, and next time will be easier! Look for people you recognize, or who have an official capacity at the event, or the presenter. These connections provide an opening for you to go up, introduce yourself, and start a conversation, even if it's just to say thank you for coming. You can also say hello to someone who is standing alone or looking lost.

Dive in, be friendly and relaxed, and before you know it, the two of you may have found something in common. Sometimes just cruise until someone catches your eye and turns to introduce himself. Even though it can feel uncomfortable until someone does, the payoff is really great. Be sure to smile—it makes you more approachable. Interacting with people is the key to business, so do it early and often!

At my level, I sometimes still see women "clumping." They tend to gravitate toward one another, rather than introducing themselves to a man. Big mistake. Sometimes I walk into an event and discover a dozen tables of men and *one* with all the women in the room crowded around it. That's terrible. In most industries, you've got to interact with men to be successful. You might as well figure out how to do it early in your career when the stakes are low. Let me restate that: interacting with *MEN* is the key to business, so do it early and do it often.

When you talk with someone during a networking event, don't make another mistake sometimes made by young businesswomen: Don't chitchat or make small talk. Remember that you've come to learn. Ask real questions and exchange substantive information, especially if you discover that the person you're talking to has a particular expertise. Keep in mind that guys like to deal in facts and figures—that will help you keep him interested and result in a meaningful conversation.

Ask specific questions about his company, background, interests, strategies, or *something.* Ask about an article you read that you don't understand—he might be able to explain it. Ask how what he does contributes to his company. Ask who their customers are and how his company finds them. If you have useful contributions to the conversation, speak up. It helps further the discussion and gives you business credibility. Most businessmen like talking about their work and themselves, so they'll probably enjoy your interaction. Before you know it, you're having a wonderful conversation that you may remember for the rest of your life.

Of course, you'll always be polite and not appear to pry, but I wouldn't err on the side of being so politically correct that you're boring. Sometimes young women are so anxious not to offend that they only offer up platitudes, and as a result, they all sound alike and not very interesting. Occasionally we confuse "professional" with "bland."

You should generally avoid personal conversations, although it's not a complete no-no. Later in your career, if your company has paid for you to attend an event, the hope is that you'll make some useful contacts, not just talk about what television shows you like. But if you've been talking to someone for a while, and the conversation slides into a discussion of your family, it's no big deal. Just don't talk about personal issues to the exclusion of more important topics. At an event like this, the impression you want to leave behind is a respectful "She's friendly, but she's all business." You're not trying to make a social friend.

Another networking skill you need is how to stop talking to one person and move on to someone else. If you're standing in a group, it's easy—you just turn to another person and introduce yourself, and usually the conversation takes off from there. If you've talked to everyone in the group that you want to (which means everybody you don't know), you can say, "I guess we're supposed to circulate," or "I think I'll go meet some other people." It's polite to do this because usually your conversational partner knows he needs to talk to other people, too; he just doesn't know how to extricate himself from you without appearing rude.

Start building your very important database of contacts while you're in school. I use an electronic database in conjunction with a business card file, and hardly a day goes by that I don't consult it. Some accomplished retired business people claim they can make a living through "contact consulting," by putting their contacts in touch with each other. In any case, it will be quite helpful to you, and increasingly so, as you progress in your career. Be sure to include personal notes that will help you remember the individual. My own notes are quite specific, but I'm sometimes transfixed by the thought that they could somehow be uploaded into the virtual world, where it will be revealed that I've used such descriptors as "peculiar" or "goofy."

Here are a few more networking tools you need:

- A solid handshake: Do shake hands when you introduce yourself, and make it a firm grip with lots of hand-to-hand contact. Don't offer a limp hand that the other person is obliged to shake himself like a wet noodle. Make sure your hand goes all the way into the other person's hand. Some men will just shake your fingers, and you should try to keep this from happening. Let him know you're not that fragile—he can shake your whole hand; you're not going to break. (Guys, if you're reading this, please quit shaking a woman's fingers, instead of her hand, at least in a business setting. It's gross.)
- A noticeable name tag: Make sure your company name is nice and big, or if you're not working yet, it says something about you like "Marketing MBA Candidate," "Graduating Class of 2020," or anything eye-catching. Guys often network with an agenda, so they may be on the hunt for someone affiliated with your company or school.
- A good memory: Focus on the other person's name when he or she offers it. You'll get better at hearing and retaining names the more you practice. This is important to locate people afterward if you haven't gotten their business card but want to keep in touch. Nowadays it's easy to find people through the social networking sites even if you only have an approximation of their name.

- Business cards: Carry them and exchange them, but don't be concerned if you didn't get or give out a lot. The purpose of networking isn't to collect business cards.

Get Out There!

Interviews are the key to advancement, so don't leave them to chance. The more preparation you have, the more confident you'll feel, and the more likely you are to go on interviews and do well. I like Martin Yates's books about job hunting, but there are many excellent ones. Consult several.

That brings us to another mistake young women who are still in school sometimes make: avoiding interviewing. Again, the excuses are usually weak: "That company isn't hiring—they're just keeping up a presence at the placement center," "I don't like talking about myself," "I know they won't hire me anyway—I'm not their type." Ha! All these excuses are actually good reasons to go and interview, just for *practice*. The more you practice, the more comfortable you'll feel, and the better you'll get at it. Then, when you get an interview at a company you really care about, you'll knock 'em dead.

Here's an example: The director of the placement center at my graduate school predicted I would struggle during the interview process. "You're too quiet and too modest," he said. He probably also meant "too unconventional and too female," but he stopped himself. I was stunned. I'd been successful at finding work before business school—were these interviews really that different? But I buckled down. I read, practiced, sought feedback, and interviewed and interviewed. Any company that invited me to their site got a visit from me—and guess what—I ended up with *fourteen* job offers. The director just laughed and shook his head when he told me I'd set a new record at the center. I was surprised and glad I'd overcome the weaknesses he'd observed.

A recruiter made an observation I'll pass along here. She said, "Once you've been invited to the interview, nothing is standing between you and the job offer. They've invited you because they think you're a match. You have the correct background, experience, education, etc. On paper, you fulfill their expectations. So, it's only up to you to blow it during the interview." That's a new perspective on what you're trying to accomplish in the interview. Make sure it's a job you want, and don't blow it.

On the other hand, when you get turned down for a job, I wouldn't worry about it. Recruiters are often very skilled at identifying candidates who will fit into their company. That's why you want to be forthright and transparent during the interview process. Don't pretend to be something you're not and try to fool the company into hiring you. If you're not a natural fit with their culture, you'll hate it there and you won't stay. Trust them to make an accurate evaluation of your style and character and objectively assess whether you'll flourish in their environment. If you get rejected, be happy—maybe they've just saved you from some horrible boss you wouldn't have been able to tolerate.

Beware, occasionally, junior business people become a bit defensive during and after the interview, so they miss an opportunity to make an even better impression. Of course, you're not over-selling during the interview—that just hinders the process. But you are gathering an extraordinary amount of information about what the company needs during your time there. Why not capitalize on that information to impress upon your potential employer that you've been listening, assimilating, and reflecting on how you might contribute? A followup thank you letter or email is a great way to do that. I sometimes hear candidates say, "Well, I'll wait to see if I get an offer before I get in touch again." Why? Is contact with you such a coveted experience that people are standing by breathlessly in hopes of stealing a rare exchange? Nope, it isn't. So, write a formal thank you letter and make some observations about what you learned and what your thoughts are. Make it meaty; don't just go through the motions. Also don't handwrite your thank you notes for interviews. If you're invited to dinner at someone's house, you can handwrite a note to the hosts, but business correspondence should be typed.

You should be getting the general drift here of my guidance: Don't be shy. Show off! Have fun! I envy you just starting out. I hope you have a thirty-year career and that in the end, you've been transformed into a revered and powerful businesswoman. This can be a fabulous adventure.

Your First Company

When you are making a decision about where you want to work, you need to know how your functional area and your gender are represented at each company, along with the usual considerations of position and salary. Reading this section will help you determine if your area of specialization is valued at the company and how to look for signs of a "glass ceiling," which will make it more difficult for you to progress rapidly. When you consider competing salary offers, it is also important to know what questions to ask about the personnel evaluation process. Finally, issues regarding size, reputation, and culture of the companies are reviewed. Although most job choices are made on the basis of location, to the extent that you have geographic flexibility, these considerations will help get you on the right path to building your A+ resume.

Who's in Charge?

Some companies are finance-driven, while others are marketing- or engineering-driven. Be sure your function is considered a priority in that company and that representatives from your department are seated on the senior strategic committees. Money and opportunity will flow down from them, and you want to be in line to receive them. Sometimes you can tell what functions are most highly-valued by looking at the background of the last few CEOs and the areas of expertise that are represented on the board of directors. You'll benefit from the training you get in companies where your function is strong, and having that company's name on your resumé will help you throughout your career.

The more you study your company, the more you will understand what strategies the company uses to remain profitable and differentiate itself from the competition. Some companies rely heavily on marketing and advertising to maintain their competitive edge. Others are distinguished by their excellent financial management and careful investments. One company might be a sales powerhouse, with an astounding distribution network throughout the globe, ready to latch onto any product that comes their way, while another focuses on unique and exquisite technology which only requires a small but highly-educated sales force to reach their niche market. Think about how your functional area contributes to the overall strength and strategy of the company. The best company for you will be one in which your functional area is considered very important.

Where Are the Girls?

You must also consider the representation of females at your target company. Are there at least one or two women at senior levels who aren't related to a founder or an owner? If there's only one woman on the board and only one senior female human resources person at the top, I'd be leery. It's not a knockout, but you might scrutinize the next level down to see if women are represented at the vice president level or if they're in charge of large numbers of employees. If there's only a smattering of women in staff or support positions, or in charge of special projects, and none in line positions (those that drive profitability), definitely hesitate. It might be very difficult to pioneer a path for women in that environment. If you're ready for that kind of challenge, and you're willing to "go first" and open the company up for women to follow behind you, good for you! But be cognizant of how tough it's going to be. You may face more than the usual amount of discrimination.

Obviously these considerations only apply in male-dominated companies. If the company you're looking at is run by women, you don't need to be concerned about that, but you're probably not reading this book in that case!

Good Choices

Suppose you're a recent graduate with a finance degree, and you're offered entry-level positions with similar salaries at two different companies. The first one is a traditional blue-suit pharmaceutical company with a token woman on the board and thin female representation at senior levels. On the other hand, several female mid-managers in your functional area have been pointed out as up-and-coming, and some of the most senior male executives have a finance background. The company is known to be finance-driven. The second company is a high-tech outfit in Silicon Valley, reputed to be a great place to work, with a non-traditional culture. There are lots of women in finance at the manager level although they're located in audit and accounting, rather than in strategic roles. Engineers and technicians hold the most senior positions, and they are exclusively male. Some board members are women although their areas of expertise don't seem to be particularly aligned with the company's core businesses. Which one do you choose?

This is a real-life example. These were the two final companies I chose between when I graduated. I selected the pharmaceutical company despite its "old boys' club" feel. The high-tech firm, although its fun culture was appealing, worried me because all the women were relegated to staff roles, and because the power in the company was clearly concentrated in engineering. As a female finance person, I was concerned I'd be sidelined and would struggle for training and opportunity.

Your choices are bound to be different and more complicated in some way or another than mine, but I hope you take the long-term view when you choose. You probably won't stay at your first company for your entire career, but if you make a good choice, your tenure may be long, and perhaps you *will* be there forever. Think about how this company's name will look on your resumé and what message it will send to your future employers about your priorities. Experienced management, good business practices, opportunity, and training should be considered along with the starting salary.

A Quantified Rating System Is Better for You

You should certainly attempt to negotiate your salary if the offer from the company you prefer is lower than others you receive, but you should also inquire about the personnel evaluation process, how frequently it occurs, how formalized it is, and whether or not a salary adjustment is typical at that time. A personnel evaluation process that includes a quantified rating system tied to salary increases is better for you because there's less room for gender discrimination. Ask what typical annual increases have been over the past few years, what bonuses you would be eligible for, and whether or not they have been paid, typically. It may turn out that a higher opening offer would be quickly surpassed by the salary at another company after a couple of years.

Large Versus Small

I would recommend that your first company be a large corporation, rather than a small company. Being hired into a Fortune 500 company gives you credibility for the rest of your career. Going through the hiring process and earning your stripes there will also give you immediate status. Large companies provide a great starting place because they invest in their new hires with training and career management. Since they've chosen you, they'll go to considerable effort to develop and prepare you for a long career at their company. Remember, your company wants you to stay and grow. They'll put you where you'll be successful because it's in their best interest. It's up to you as the years go by to decide if you want to stay or not, but don't overlook the advantages a large corporation offers you.

In addition, large companies have usually worked hard to establish good corporate practices that will be beneficial to learn. You can learn now what a good employee handbook looks like, what fair personnel policies are, objective ways to establish roles and responsibilities, logical titles, what a balanced organizational chart looks like, and so forth. That will help you throughout your career, especially when you need to deal with these issues when you have a more senior role. Large companies have the resources to devote to personnel issues and get them right. This can set a high standard for you and give you a solid foundation to build on.

American Versus Non-American

At the risk of being politically incorrect, I'd suggest that you join an American company if you're an American woman looking for work in the U.S. There is discrimination in corporate America, but the percentage of women in senior positions is still highest at American companies. Canadian and British companies aren't far behind, and I enjoyed working for a British firm for a number of years, but be aware that if the company's culture is very different from a typical American business, you'll look like an alien and struggle to fit in. I'd particularly hesitate to join a company headquartered in Asia where working women are still a minority. There may be exceptions, but make sure you start out with a healthy dose of skepticism before you're convinced to take a job at a non-American company.

What They Claim Versus What's Visible

During the interview process, I wouldn't ask directly about opportunities for women. Since the results are pretty visible, you can see for yourself how the company is doing. And reality is likely to be different from any official response you'll receive. I wouldn't pay much attention to any claims by the company that they're "gender-blind." Nobody is truly gender-neutral; it's just something they've been told to say. It's easy to avoid companies that have a history of sex discrimination lawsuits, but some places appear to offer good opportunities when, in fact, they don't. Some companies have programs designed to promote women or have put considerable effort (and expense) into marketing themselves as a "good place to work for women," but the results just aren't there when you look at representation at the senior levels. Think of how long professional women have been entering the workforce—at least three decades, right? If there are opportunities for women at that company, you should be seeing some at the top. Here's another time you can practice putting on your skeptical spectacles and your critical-thinking cap in the corporate world. There will be lots more!

I wouldn't want your questions to raise any flags about you as though you could be a "problem." It's unfortunate, but companies are so worried about legal issues that it might compromise your candidacy if they think they're hiring a whiner or someone who might eventually sue. I would take note of all gender issues, but I wouldn't talk about them to company employees. Obviously, you'll make your own decisions based on your particular circumstances, but I would start with this very safe approach.

The Cubette

Now, let's talk about your life as a junior person in the company—a new hire. Your highest priority will be the nuts and bolts of your job, and I encourage you to soak up all the training, advice, and experience that you can. There's much to learn, and your brain is likely to feel completely full each night when you go home! Be sure not to miss out on learning opportunities or chances to gain exposure because you're spending too much time working on your specific projects. For you to progress, you need to be visible, and your managers need to know what you're working on. First jobs can present special pitfalls for women, from dealing with junior male employees to office politics. In this section, we'll also discuss the decision-making process when you are contemplating a move to another company.

Learning How To

Now is a great time to attend every seminar and training course your company offers *before* you have larger responsibilities that make you wish you'd learned some of these skills earlier. So, be a sponge, grab every opportunity, don't be too picky about your assignments, and start building your arsenal of skills. Here are some topics you can explore at this level (and they'll help you during your entire career): interviewing and hiring, supervision and delegation, personnel evaluations, discrimination and sexual harassment, negotiating, fraud prevention, time management, setting and measuring goals, layoffs and terminations, quality improvement, effective meetings, first aid and CPR (you never know!).

Seminars that include role-play allow you to practice in a safe environment which is quite helpful because it often turns out to be harder to put difficult communication into words once you're in the real-life situation. Seminars that cover the legal aspects of these topics are valuable as well. Personnel management has become very technical, and it's helpful to know what your legal boundaries are. If your company doesn't offer these workshops internally, ask if you can attend them on the outside. Even if you aren't yet supervising people, it shows you're preparing yourself for the next level.

Just Go

Because young businesswomen are very serious about building their careers, they sometimes make the mistake of sticking to their knitting when they should be more visible and spending more time building relationships. I've said it before, but I'll say it again: Business means interacting with people, and in most companies, that means interacting with men. Don't make the mistake of staying in your cubicle when you should be getting out.

If your boss asks you to go to lunch, always go. He represents your most important relationship at work, and time spent with him is never wasted. There's a tremendous amount you can learn from your boss, and outside of the office, he may have more inclination and time to spend talking to you about the business. Ask him about current business news; his experience will make his perspective and insight very informative. It's also a chance for him to get to know you a bit, which is a good thing.

Go to meetings. I know most are terribly run and seem like a waste of time. But you can't contribute properly to your organization if you're not present when decisions are being made. If nothing else, you'll learn more about your company and colleagues.

In particular, if you're lucky enough to get invited to a meeting where the participants are more senior than you, definitely go. Somehow this seems counter-intuitive to many junior business people, but these meetings allow you to perform in front of your superiors, those who will influence your career progression. And presumably, you'll do well and make a great impression. You'll figure out the best way to behave at these meetings when you've been invited as a junior attendee, but being a good listener and offering a comment at the end is a fine starting place. If it turns out you know quite a bit about the topic the senior staff is discussing, don't be afraid to speak up. It could be that's why you were invited. You just don't want to dominate the conversation. If your boss is attending, it would be wise to clarify with him beforehand how he would like you to participate.

Think about whom you'll have access to when you're invited somewhere. If you're invited to recruit at a college campus, and you'll be traveling on the company jet with the CEO and a senior human resources person, be smart and *go*!

Sports Idioms

If you're working with men, I suggest you become a fan of sports idioms. If they don't come naturally to you, don't throw in the towel—go check them out on Wikipedia. I don't recall if I started using them right off the bat, or if I use them now because they're just par for the course. They're a cliché in business, but why *wouldn't* you learn them, so you can handle a few curve balls? Perhaps as Title IX funding develops more female athletes, sports-oriented language and concepts will make it easier for women to get in the game. I played softball, and baseball expressions were in my wheelhouse, but it's a bit hit or miss with other older women.

Office Politics

Depending on your company, this may be where you get your first taste of politics. I'd love to say you won't see any in corporate America, but probably anywhere human beings are interacting, politics exist. Definitions vary, but here's mine: Politics are in action whenever something happens that shouldn't have happened according to proper organizational behavior or processes. If an employee tries to curry favor with her manager because he's friends with her dad, that's politics. If a group of employees gang up on some poor soul because she went to an ivy-league school, that's politics. If someone gets a position or an assignment because the boss is playing favorites, rather than making an objective assessment of a person's qualifications, that's politics. It's not right. It's not fair. But it happens all the time.

I find politics are strongest in companies with a weak CEO who makes too many decisions based on favoritism or other non-objective criteria. The real reasons behind these decisions are often obvious to the rest of the company, and the jockeying for an influential position around the CEO that ensues can be very dysfunctional. Unfortunately, egotistical CEOs often enjoy the scrabbling and in-fighting that goes along with this kind of screwed-up environment and ignore the damage it's doing to the company. Company politics are irritating to watch and painful to endure.

Politics occur at all levels, including at the board of directors' level. Inexperienced board members don't trust their own decisions, so they curtail due process and may be overly swayed by a forceful personality. Similarly, bad managers who aren't tough enough to apply the rules fairly and equally let some employees get away with misbehavior to the detriment of all employees. In these environments, arrogant and aggressive employees may dominate because their managers are afraid of them. Employees who flatter and fawn over their managers may also move into inappropriate positions of power. These employees aren't pulling their weight and contributing to the corporate process by hard work, valuable input, and feedback—they're simply stroking the boss's ego.

How are *you* going to rise above these kinds of shenanigans and not get sucked into political games? First, think about the organizational chart. This document lays out objectively who has the authority to decide what. The corresponding job descriptions define roles and responsibilities and, by implication, the qualifications of the people who hold those positions. These can be used to define perquisites like company cars, office sizes, budgets, support positions and other issues that tend to become controlled by office politics. Try to be a good corporate citizen, and use objective criteria to make decisions, give rewards, and allocate resources. If policies about travel, club memberships, associations, and social events are transparent and defined, associated politics just disappear. You can't eradicate politics, but you can minimize the most obvious issues.

If you're the victim of politics, you should talk to your manager about what happened in case there was something about the situation that you missed. If somebody took a shortcut and didn't go through proper channels, or bypassed normal procedures, you can point out objectively what *should* have happened and emphasize how the situation could be handled correctly in the future. But sometimes, unfair things happen.

As you grow more experienced, you'll become more attuned to political undercurrents, and as you grow more powerful, you'll find ways of stopping unfair politics and creating better outcomes. Listening, observing, and gaining the confidence of your co-workers will arm you with the knowledge you need to cut off political behavior before it's damaging. Being politically savvy will help you and your company be more successful, but you don't have to engage in unfair behaviors yourself. You can be politically astute without playing dirty office politics.

Dealing with Stupid Stuff

Women sometimes react very negatively to comments made by their male colleagues. And, I know, guys can say really stupid things sometimes. On the other hand, occasionally I hear examples of some "terrible thing" a guy said, and I think, "So what?" Some guys are just awkward, not malevolent. Many guys don't know how to compliment women they work with, and you may have to give them the benefit of the doubt. Many are unaccustomed to working with women as their peers, and they're figuring it out as they go. They may have good intentions—their comments just come out poorly. So, don't be defensive. If he says, "You come across really well; your appearance is very professional," don't say to yourself, "Well! He wouldn't have commented on a *man's* appearance!" Or if he says, "Wow! You were like Angelina Jolie in that meeting!" don't react to the female superhero image. If it's positive, take it as positive.

Don't get me wrong, there are jerks out there. Some guys can be quite nasty and try to cloak their put-downs under the guise of "I'm just kidding." But I find it more productive to ignore these jokers than call them on their dumb behavior. If someone makes a pointed, unpleasant comment about your appearance, or your weight, or some other sensitive topic, let it roll off your back. You're bigger than he is. This also signals to the rest of your colleagues you're really too busy to deal with a nincompoop.

In a similar vein, many women have asked me how they're supposed to interpret a man's behavior when he opens the office door for you. Should they be insulted and refuse to walk through the door? Gee. I think most guys hold the door for you because they've been told that's what they're supposed to do and that it's *polite*. So, just walk through, and say thank you. When it's more graceful for you to hold the door for him, do it. He may put his hand above yours on the door and take over the door-holding so you can go ahead, but that's okay—he just really wants to hold the door for you. Ladies, this is not a big deal. Salaries, promotions, sexual harassment, immoral behavior—those are big deals. Door opening is not.

Mentors, Sponsors, and Coaches

I prefer to think of your manager as your mentor, but many companies today have formal mentoring programs. I'd take advantage of them, but I'd try to get a male mentor, rather than a female one. Not that you won't get great advice from a female mentor (clearly I thought you might or I wouldn't have written this book!), but a male mentor may be better able to explain specific situations in your particular company. You're trying to become incorporated into a male environment, not run a separate track through it.

Sponsors take the mentoring relationship one step further by taking action on your behalf, instead of just advising you. They may recommend you for an opportunity, enroll you in a special program, or get you assigned to a cross-functional committee. You're very lucky if someone steps up to sponsor you, and it doesn't matter if they're male or female.

You may also be offered an opportunity to work with an external coach, and in most cases, you should grab it. Your company could be paying for this resource because you have a specific developmental need, or you might be participating as part of a broader program. Ask what the goals are of the coaching program, and make sure they coincide with your needs. Coaches can be amazingly insightful and very skillful at working with you in subtle ways that won't hurt your feelings and will improve your confidence, outlook, and performance. Good coaches can offer golden nuggets of advice that you'll treasure the rest of your career. However, some companies use coaches as change agents; that is, the coaching program has an agenda, more or less hidden, to institute a cultural change in the organization. It may still be helpful for you to participate in a program like that, but naturally the program's goals will be more focused on the needs of the corporation than on your professional development.

Moving On

Even though you've just started in your new company, let's spend a couple of minutes thinking about how to leave and how to avoid some potential pitfalls. If you *do* think about leaving (and what new employee doesn't during the first year, especially after she's just gotten her first dose of office politics?), don't act rashly. You don't want to make the mistake of leaving for a worse situation. If you did a good job selecting your first company, you've invested considerable research and energy in that decision. Don't walk away from that without a good reason. A decent tenure (two years is ideal) in your first position out of school will look good on your resumé for the rest of your career. Too often, I see young employees' pride causes them to act self-destructively for the long term by leaving a position too soon.

Nonetheless, if you do begin seriously thinking about leaving, and even tacitly looking for another position, here are some ideas to keep in mind. Don't tell your current company you're thinking of leaving. After all, you may change your mind depending on what you find. And your manager can't do much with that information except watch you and worry, or start moving responsibilities away from you in anticipation of your departure.

Don't use your potential departure as a threat, as in, "If you don't give me more money, I'm quitting." What if your managers don't give you any more money, but you can't find a position you like better? Then you just look weak, and you've lost whatever negotiating power such a threat offered, if any. If you want more money, ask for more money. If you want a higher-level position, ask for it. If they think you're worth it, they'll get you what you want, or show their interest in keeping you in some way. If they don't, they know what they risk—you don't have to rub it in.

When you're in a junior position, don't leave until you have a new position lined up. It's a major drawback to be looking for work when you're unemployed. I understand it's difficult to stay focused on your current job and keep your job search a secret, but remember, there's no crime in looking, and you may decide to stay where you are. Sometimes merely looking helps you recognize some benefits to your current position compared with the rest of the marketplace.

Keep this in mind for the future, when you discover one of *your* employees is looking around a bit. It's not a crisis, and probably he or she should get a taste of the market from time to time. They might end up staying right where they are, so you shouldn't take it as a personal affront.

Do talk to all the recruiters who call you. Even if they have a position you wouldn't take if hell froze over, you may know someone who would be a good candidate, and you want to make a favorable impression in hopes that they'll put a positive note about you in their database. Relationships with recruiters can be incredibly valuable, not only for finding work, but for giving career advice and explaining hiring trends, salary surveys, the current employment market, and how you fit in. Some recruiters have known me for twenty years and have essentially watched me grow up. Their intelligent observations and objective feedback have helped my career enormously. Plus, they have fabulous networks and often know what's going on all over town.

If you do leave, do so in as upbeat a way as you can. Emphasize the positive aspects of where you're going, not the negatives of the company you're leaving. In particular, don't badmouth your current company to employees who are staying behind. How's that supposed to make them feel? Say goodbye and thank you to your managers. Leave your work in order, or if possible, do a good job training your replacement so that he or she doesn't struggle after you've left. You don't want to burn bridges with the company or your colleagues. The business world is surprisingly small, and your great reputation should trail behind you and precede you when you're on the move.

Keep Playing

Remember the video game you started playing at the beginning of your career? At every step along your development path, you should be aware of what skills you're gaining to put on your tool belt. You get to carry that tool belt with you every time you change jobs, and the addition of every tool will make you more valuable to your new employer. Focus on *learning* and growing professionally.

Ask your manager what skills she or he thinks you should develop that would benefit your company. Be open-minded. At this stage, any special assignment offers a chance to learn something new. You may have to ask for specific opportunities or assignments to develop particular tactical skills. Be nice about it and understand that the company wants to develop you, but your manager also needs to get work out of you. If you ask for something and your company can't grant it right away, be patient. If your manager knows you're ambitious, he or she will likely arrange something for you that's a little different. If you're offered a challenge that's bigger than you expected, don't back away. Have some faith that you'll figure it out. Don't be afraid to stretch and try new things.

If I'd Only Known...

These early days of your career are likely to bring you the fondest memories of your work life although they can also be very challenging. Everyone has a list of "things I wish I'd known back then." Remember though that the level of discomfort you feel from navigating new situations early in your career will diminish as you gain confidence. Positive behavior will become more automatic as you begin to "own" your corporate identity. In addition, as you work and grow and become a better manager, you're educating your male colleagues about how effective a businesswoman can be—so, you're doing good on many levels.

CHAPTER FOUR

Navigation Tips

THE CORPORATE WORLD CAN LOOK LIKE a real thicket when you're being advised don't do this, don't do that, change this, and so forth. What are the positive aspects that you can fall back on and be confident about, without feeling as though you're committing some *other* mistake? In this chapter, we'll start with some guiding lights to follow and then talk specifically about how to deal positively with three areas that are often difficult for executive women: competition, challenge, and conflict.

Guiding Lights

Because you will see discrimination and injustice, you need a positive set of beliefs to ground you during your career. Following are seven truths you can count on that will guide your behavior so that, even when your workplace seems unfair, you can think rationally about it. This allows you to persevere and do your best every day, knowing your professionalism and smarts will ultimately be rewarded.

Truth #1: Cream Rises to the Top

I was fortunate to work for a great boss when I first ventured into the business world. He was smart, fierce, challenging, and attentive. He was a tall Armenian with bushy eyebrows, and the other analysts and I called him Darth behind his back and would alert each other by breathing down the phone when he was on his way. I was half-terrified of him.

"No!" he would bristle when I showed him my financial spreadsheets. "That's not what I thought. I don't believe you!"

"Um, but I think I'm right?" I would quaver, and after I countered every challenge and offered enough examples explaining why I thought I was right, he would growl, "Okay." Presented with enough evidence, he was willing to change his position. Or maybe he was just checking. You can't ask for more than that in a boss, and all the analysts flourished under him.

In contrast, there was another manager in the office with whom we interacted but didn't report to. He was quite a contrast: lacking in analytical skills or people smarts, he relied on humiliation and snarkyness to dominate his employees. He sometimes bragged he'd made every woman who reported to him cry at least once. One woman who worked with him, a professional, even-tempered, and good-humored person, told me in complete seriousness, that if she were ever given an opportunity to kill someone and get away with it, she would pick him. "I would do it with a hammer," she said.

So my heart sank when my wonderful boss appeared in my doorway one day to tell me he was being transferred and we would now all report to Eyeballs (we had other names for him, but I'll use a fairly mild one here). Somehow my manager knew that this was horrifying news to me because, confronted by my faltering "But…," he replied, "Look, Jennifer, just remember, cream rises to the top." In time, in almost all companies, that's true, and it's worthwhile to keep in mind when things happen that make no sense.

Eventually, he was right. Not to say we didn't struggle. My colleagues hated working for Eyeballs. He got that particular nickname after a typo was found in a financial schedule, and instead of intelligently thinking about how the mistake had occurred, he decided to throw "more eyeballs" at the problem and insisted *every* analyst in the group proofread *every* schedule from then on. It was mind-numbing and ineffective; we never caught another error that way, and it took up days of our time.

Even worse was how mean he was. One of my teammates was a quiet, amiable man, but following another sarcastic and demeaning phone conversation with Eyeballs, he said to me, "I hate that guy!" and violently drove his pencil straight through an apple sitting on his desk. I got along with Eyeballs a little better than my colleagues, but he was a pain to deal with. He had an uncomfortable relationship with his wife and would sigh after he got off the phone with her, "Don't ever get married, Jennifer." But unlike my colleagues, I could see he wasn't all bad. I sometimes thought his snide comments were funny, and you certainly couldn't accuse him of being politically correct. Nevertheless, when it came time for the employee survey, everyone let him have it.

There were two questions on the survey regarding your manager: one dealing with his skills as a manager, and one relating to his overall competence. Every person in his department rated him a 0 out of 5 on both questions. Everyone. So, when they tell you a survey is anonymous, keep in mind it's only anonymous as long as it isn't *unanimous*.

I wasn't very happy to receive a phone call from Eyeballs after the results of the survey had been shared with him. I'd been transferred out of his department by then, so he probably felt it was okay to call me. He was heart-broken. "Why?" he asked. I tried to be kind and offer some suggestions, but it wasn't long before he wasn't with the company any more. The rumor was he took a job as controller for a chicken farm, which brought joyful snickers from my colleagues.

Keep the big picture in mind and let things play out. It's hard when you're in the thick of it, but remember you're going to have a long career, and you may look back on this and laugh. A year working for a terrible boss, or in a hopeless division, or following some foolish, laughable procedure may turn out to be more educational than you realize at the time. Another good manager said to me, "Jennifer, don't sweat it. In two years, this won't matter, and in five years, no one will even remember you worked here." It's a bit cavalier, but it did help me put in perspective some petty cash variance I was battling at the time.

This will help you be philosophical about any minor setbacks in your career. Say you didn't get the promotion you wanted after twelve months, is that really a crisis? Are you willing to wait a little longer? If yes, then don't over-react. If you're enjoying your position and learning a lot, be patient. Maybe they just need to season you a bit more. Think carefully before you switch jobs just because you're miffed. If you're good, your company will recognize it soon enough. Cream rises to the top.

Truth #2: This Is a Business Relationship

Don't be starry-eyed about money. You work; they pay you. So, don't undersell your work. Ask for a salary that will make you excited to go work there. If someone else has offered you more, tell them. Say, "I really want to come work for you, but the salary isn't what I hoped. Do you have any flexibility?" Maybe they can make something up to you in a sign-on bonus if they can't move the starting salary. Don't worry about offending anyone. Just be honest and open-minded. Negotiate with integrity. If they give you what you ask for, take the job. Don't play games, and then ask for something more.

Don't assume life's fair and you'll get what you deserve. Actually, you will get what you deserve for such foolish thinking, and that means less than you would if you looked up some competitive salary information. Do your homework and research what typical salaries are at your level. Once you've presented that information, and they've said that's as high as they can go, either take it and drop the discussion, or go someplace else. At that point, assume you're paid exactly what you're worth to the company; don't be fooled into thinking you're worth more. If you can make more elsewhere, think about leaving. It's a business relationship. It's not personal.

I've been surprised to hear even human resource professionals assume a woman is satisfied with her salary if they haven't heard otherwise. Several times I've had to question why no salary adjustment was being made for a woman at year-end when an increase was given to men in the same department. "She's happy," was the response. How do they know she's happy? "Well, she hasn't said anything."

Salary negotiations are definitely not all roses. I remember asking a boss for a pay raise, which he not only refused but then brought up several times afterward in front of others to mock my apparently inflated opinion of my worth. It embarrassed me, but I had enough experience by then to recognize he was being a doofus, and I left that company eventually (for more money). In retrospect, I suspect he'd never had the experience of having a woman ask for more money and was probably shocked.

I counsel my employees not to get altruistic about their employment. Every time they give up a holiday, or work late on their daughter's birthday, or some other sacrifice, without knowing it, they put a chip in the credit account they mentally keep in their heads related to the company. The company, however, is blithely unaware of this running total, and eventually, if the employee gives up too much family time or makes too many sacrifices, he or she snaps and quits, and *everyone* loses: the company and the employee. I encourage employees to keep a balanced account—sometimes the company does something nice for you; sometimes you do something nice for the company. Since your personal sacrifices are within your control, don't let them get out of synch. Ultimately, it's too expensive. You may think you're indispensable and that the company couldn't survive without you, but it probably doesn't share your view, so don't turn yourself into a martyr. It's a harsh but important lesson for young employees to learn early in their career.

Truth #3: You Have to Ask for What You Want

In my talks with various female colleagues over the years, I was sometimes mystified by their reticence to make their desires known. They were perfectly willing to clearly explain to me why they should be promoted, or have a new responsibility, or be given a raise, but when I would say, "Well, what does your boss say?" they would turn coy and waffle about it. They wanted to assume that decisions were made based on merit and that they shouldn't have to ask for what's just fair. "Strange," I'd say to myself, "Sure, it may not be a comfortable conversation but not to have it at all? That's crazy." In my observation, this is especially pronounced in younger women. Since they've been told there's no gender discrimination anymore, they don't realize they have to ask for what they deserve.

I've spent some time thinking about why I forced myself to ask for what I wanted. It wasn't easy, but somehow I knew I had to, and I bet I know who's to blame—my dad.

"What's the harm in asking?" he would say. "They can just say no."

I heard that over and over, so I did ask: to volunteer at the library when I was way too young to be a volunteer, for special projects in school, to go to public school in Switzerland when it was against the rules, to attend graduate level courses in my undergrad program, for independent study, for a grant from the Dean's office to go to a conference, for a transfer to a new division, for an overseas opportunity... These were all requests where the answer was yes. I'm sure there were others where I was told no, but I just kept asking.

My dad gave me some early coaching about how to ask for jobs, money, and opportunities, and I got a lot of practice. He told me how to get my first job when I was fourteen.

"Go down the street and go into every store and ask them for a job. It doesn't matter if they have an opening or not. Just go ask!" He described how you negotiate in good faith for what you think is fair pay. He drove home the point that showing initiative is a positive indication of what kind of worker you'll be. As I thought through these lessons, I realized I'd put them into action at an early age, then practiced them for the next forty years. I wasn't braver or smarter than other women; I just got more practice!

A former colleague who has gone into academia refers to working business people as "practitioners," which I thought was pretty funny until it dawned on me that we *are* practitioners—we practice and practice every day, in order to get better at our jobs!

Asking for opportunities is difficult, but the sooner you start practicing, the sooner you'll feel (more) comfortable doing it. Recognize that your managers may say no to your requests (in fact, they're likely to say no), but at least they know what you want, and if an opportunity arises in the future, they may be able to accommodate your wishes. As a manager, I found it harder *not* knowing what my employees' aspirations were and feeling as though I might be dragging a higher level of ambition out of them than they were comfortable with.

Life is more negotiable than you might think. When I discovered that a company I'd just joined had been underpaying its taxes for a number of years, we got in touch with the tax department and set up a phone call to explain what had happened. We assumed we'd have to pay back taxes, interest, and presumably a heavy fine. I'll never forget the look on my accounting manager's face when the person from the tax department said to us, "Well, how much *can* you pay?" It turned into a negotiation. We ended up paying a fraction of what we owed—the authorities were probably so startled someone would come forward and volunteer to pay delinquent taxes that they took pity on us. If taxes are negotiable, everything is negotiable!

Truth #4: But Be Creative and *Patient* about Negotiating

Sometimes men see negotiation as black and white, but there's more than one way to reach an agreement. It's not always a win-lose proposition, and women are often naturally skilled at reaching a positive outcome both parties are happy with. Once I participated in a negotiation seminar where the role-play was "rigged," in that, unbeknownst to us, there was a possible win-win solution—if we could just discover it. My negotiation partner and I arrived at an easy solution because he only wanted the by-product of a material my company was producing, something that we were just throwing away. Our negotiation was over in two minutes. As we sat quietly and listened to the other teams getting hostile and raising their voices around us, he said, "You know, we wouldn't have figured this out if you hadn't asked me *why* I wanted that material." There's enormous value in stepping to "their" side when you're negotiating. Listen, acknowledge, agree, try to see it from their point of view—it's just common sense.

Attack the problem together. Don't treat it like it's life or death. Be cheerful and optimistic. Use humor, and don't act like your family's honor is on the line. Everyone needs to get out of this with their self-respect and integrity intact. Don't make someone lose face to close the deal.

Be patient! If it takes 10 sessions, it takes 10 sessions. Just stay with it. The best negotiator I ever worked with was also one of the most patient people I've ever met. He talked slowly, he clarified, he reiterated, he wasn't concerned with using clichés. He said, "I hear what you're saying" so many times, I thought I would freak out and run out the door shrieking. But he got deals done.

Truth #5: Work Is Funny

Work is funny-weird, but it's also funny-haha. Humor is an extremely useful tool in the workplace, particularly when working with men. Men often see the humor in things that happen at work, and you should laugh along with them. I sometimes see women being too serious at work and not very fun to be around because of their ultra-professionalism. Man: "How many feminists does it take to change a lightbulb?" Woman: "THAT'S NOT FUNNY!" Don't let that be you. Go ahead and chuckle. It will relax you and help keep work in perspective.

Learn to tell a few jokes, even if you're not a big joke teller. There have been many occasions in my career when the guys have started telling jokes, and I was glad to have a couple in my pocket. Don't just sit there like a humorless bump when jokes are going around. Don't you want to defy the "Women can't tell jokes" stereotype? I sure did. Plus there are so many great ones out there. I wouldn't tell mean or insensitive jokes, or any that put women down, but I wouldn't err on the side of being too politically correct either. Guys like it when you take some risks, so don't be too "proper." Here's one to get you started:

A successful businessman met with his new son-in-law to tell him that he was making him a 50-50 partner in his company in order to welcome him to the family. "All you have to do is come to the factory every day and learn the operations," he said. "Oh, no," said the son-in-law, "I hate factories. I can't stand the noise." "Okay," said the father-in-law, "you can work in the office and learn the corporate side." "Oh, no," said the son-in-law, "I can't stand being stuck behind a desk all day." "Wait," said the father-in-law, "I've just made you half-owner of my company, but you don't like factories or office work? What am I going to do with you?" "Easy," said the young man, "Buy me out."

I like to develop Top 10 lists when people leave my department and read them at the going-away party. "Top 10 Reasons Robert Is

Leaving Us: Reason #10: His new company has an even more screwed-up budget process than ours, and he loves a challenge. Reason #9: He wants a longer commute to work. Reason #8: He snapped after the lunchroom ran out of Doritos last Friday..." You get the idea, I hope. The more specific and closer they are to the truth (particularly if there's a sly nod to the *real* reasons), the more they serve to bond the group, remember the good times and bad, and help everyone let go.

You might be surprised at what you can get away with. I came back into my office one day to discover several members of my staff literally hiding behind my desk. It turns out they'd made *and shown* a videotape to the whole company, mocking the CEO's vanity. I couldn't believe it. The CEO was right on my heels, and he raised his eyebrows and shook his finger at them, but he laughed too, and no one got fired. Whew!

Sometimes I laugh when others would get angry. If something is ridiculous, I laugh because—well, it's ridiculous. One time, a division controller came to tell me he'd made an error in the budget he'd submitted to me. He was so nervous that he almost couldn't talk.

"How much?" I asked.

"A million dollars," he whispered.

I laughed.

"I can't believe you're laughing," he said relaxing slightly.

"Well, that's just crazy," I said, "First, I don't believe it's true—the numbers weren't that far off. Second, if it's true, we have to fix it, we can't just accept that. We'll figure it out."

Laughing doesn't mean you're not a serious person, and it's an excellent way to defuse a tense situation and build camaraderie.

Truth #6: Nobody Died

Everyone is guilty of losing perspective from time to time, but I sometimes see women fall into a trap of overreacting to events at work. Every little issue becomes a crisis because they're so anxious to do a good job. Keep the big picture in mind and ask yourself, "Did anybody die?" No. Okay then, take a deep breath and focus on what needs to happen. Few events at work are truly a crisis, and if you expend energy wastefully, it will be hard for you to keep your stamina up. Guys want to see you're tough enough to rise above small problems and can put them in perspective. Nobody likes working with someone for whom everything is a huge drama, and leaders need to show that they can absorb big blows and keep on trucking.

Truth #7: [And, finally, the big one] Don't Be Emotional at Work

The biggest complaint about working with women is that they're too emotional. If you have a reserved and stoic nature, count your blessings, but many of us are reactive, wear our heart on our sleeve, and respond to tough situations with tears. I don't know how else to say this: *You can't cry at work.* Ladies, you just can't. And although I would love to say, "There's no crying in business," unfortunately, there's *lots* of crying in business. Sometimes I felt as though every woman who walked into my office was planning a good cry. It's really a shame to see that women are so unhappy at work that the moment you offer them a kind word, they break down. That's a sad commentary on how uncomfortable they are. Nevertheless, you can't cry at work and keep your dignity. Practice taking the emotion out of a situation by focusing on the message or the problem. It's easier said than done—I know—but again, if you practice *not* crying, you'll get better at it and become proud you don't resort to this when you're upset.

From the earliest days of your career, if you have a tendency to cry when you're frustrated, angry, or hurt, you'll have to practice other reactions. I've been known to slam things around. Not that I'm proud of that (or of the language I use when I'm doing it), but it doesn't condemn me to the damning label of "emotional." When you're working with guys, some emotional reactions are acceptable, and some are not. It's not right; it's not logical; it's just how it is. Repeat after me: You can't cry at work.

Here's the issue: For men, crying signifies a loss of control. For women, it's just an indication of a powerful emotional response, which isn't necessarily bad. For men, loss of control is inherently bad. It's a weakness that's unacceptable in a senior manager. For women, it's a sign you're human. The two genders come at this from different vantage points. I understand and respect both perspectives, but, Ladies, if you're working in a man's environment, you have to conform to his rules, and that means "No crying." Honestly, I think once you get used to it, you'll be glad your emotions aren't as evident and you'll appreciate the protection that shield offers you.

I don't wish to imply that yelling is a good substitute. Clearly there's lots of yelling in business because that's mostly what guys do, but that's pretty bad too, at least for a woman. People react very negatively to the image of an angry screaming woman. If your employees or co-workers can tell your emotions are ruling your head, there's going to be hell to pay. Subordinates don't want to see this. They fear your loss of self-control means either you shouldn't be in charge of the company, or things are worse than they seem. And things always seem really bad to employees. It's stunning what they think up to worry about. Speaking of which, don't *ever* yell at your employees. It makes no sense—to holler at the people who make you successful. For shame. That's abusive and low-down.

The one time when I would reluctantly say it's okay to yell is when you're being yelled at by a bully. You don't want to lose your head and go out of control, but you may need to raise your voice to show him you're not intimidated. We'll get to how to deal with bullies later.

The Big C's: Competition, Challenge, and Conflict

Here are three more areas that executive women typically find difficult. The way we have been socialized makes us approach the Big C's differently from men, and when we are working in a man's world, their behavior can appear formidable and confusing. I attempt here to shed a little light on their attitudes and offer some suggestions for you to try.

Compete Positively

Some women have misunderstood the "game" analogies that are used to talk about the corporate world. They've come away with the idea that they need to "beat" men in order to be successful. I think it's just the opposite. To participate productively as part of a corporate team, women need to work well with men, not try to overcome them. Women need to be comfortable not only working with and reporting to men, but having men report to them. They need to understand, respect, and mentor men—not carry an antagonistic attitude toward them.

I've seen women be quite mean to male peers and adopt an adversarial stance that's completely inappropriate. They act as though they're under attack and are going to lose something if they let down their hostile guard. They withhold information, treat their partners with suspicion, and gnash their teeth if someone else gets an opportunity or a promotion. This is craziness. Your corporate colleagues are on *your* side; you need to support them, help them, and relish their accomplishments. The team's success is your success. Business endeavors are a group effort. Competitive one-upmanship works *against* the company.

There is an element of competition when it comes to advancement, but let's talk about the right way to compete. It's incorrect to denigrate your peers in hopes that will get you a promotion. Making life hard for your colleagues will only get you a reputation for being difficult to work with, which is not what you want. Promotions go to people who are *great* to work with and who have shown they can work with different kinds of people, including difficult ones. Someone with outstanding interpersonal skills is worth moving up in the organization where she can have increased influence. Being uncooperative at work only ensures that the people who have to work with you are more likely to be promoted!

The better strategy is to excel: Do great work, have a super attitude, try to work productively with everybody, and be a positive force within your company. In fact, your goal should be to make everyone around you more successful than they've been. Try to draw out the best from people, including your team members, peer group, and people who are potential candidates for the same positions you are. Think how this works: If everyone has this terrific mindset, all the team members are motivated to get more and more done, and the company benefits enormously! That's what a good corporate team looks like. They may be competing, but they're competing by trying to make the team and all its members better and better. That's why you should be happy when one of your peers gets a promotion. It means your team is hot stuff.

I've always been mystified by my co-workers who got mad when someone else got a promotion. That reaction was foreign to me, especially when the promotion went to someone in a different department or was clearly deserved. You're unhappy because someone has moved up into a job with bigger responsibilities and a bigger salary? That's just weird. But it's common. Don't fall prey to this kind of silliness. Actually, once businesswomen catch on to this idea of positive competition, I find them frequently to be extremely skilled, much better than their male peers, at seeing the workplace as a place where everyone can be a winner. Sometimes men have trouble not turning all interactions into win-lose scenarios.

Negative feelings are more understandable when two people are vying for an open position, and one gets it and the other doesn't. It's logical in that case to be disappointed if you didn't get the job, but you should still be gracious to the person who got it, and you still have to support the decision. Here's how you do it (it's pretty simple): You walk up to the person, and you say, "Congratulations. Good for you. I'm really proud of you." That's it! You don't need to talk behind the person's back, whine about it, or stab the person in the back—none of that. You say it, and you're done.

The person who was promoted will be very relieved by your acceptance of the outcome and might almost fall down in gratitude. Your superiors will notice your mature response and make a mental note that your professionalism is a sign of someone who's ready for the next level. You should have a conversation with your manager about what drove the decision and how you can be more ready the next time an opportunity comes around. Listen carefully and be reasonable. If he tells you the person who was promoted has one more year of experience than you, don't ignore that. That's a legitimate explanation. If he provides more subtle feedback that seems performance-related, don't get defensive, but do try to get clarity. If he's picking up on something that will hold you back, now is the time to fix it. See if you can get him to be fairly direct with you by rephrasing what he says in more concrete terms and by suggesting types of training or coaching that would have made you a better candidate. This is useful, and having it come early in your career is actually a benefit. I know it's hard to see it that way, but competing with someone who's better than you can highlight areas where you can improve.

In my experience, head-to-head competitive situations with one loser and one winner are rare. Sometimes opportunities are created for strong performers, so even if you didn't get this job, there might be another one right behind it. Sometimes companies will enhance someone's title or responsibilities when there's not a pre-existing position that the strong performer is ready for. In my experience, titles and positions are somewhat fluid, and companies will try to keep good performers. Focus on excelling, not competing.

Get Tough-Minded about Challenges

My dad used to say, "You should encourage questions when you give a presentation. It gives you a chance to show off." Yet women occasionally exhibit hostility when their proposals are challenged. Both men and women sometimes complain if a peer asks a question, as though there's some unspoken rule against it. A good company won't tolerate this kind of attitude. We all need to be questioned and have our ideas tested and scrutinized. That's how we arrive at good decisions.

Men often profess great faith in the power of logic. If a proposal smacks of emotion or irrationality, they'll criticize it. To be persuasive, your arguments need to be based on a logical progression of rational thought. Guys like to deal in facts, data, and results. When your conclusions are being questioned, don't get defensive. You'll get the most mileage out of what's known and provable. Theories, hypothetical discourse, and hand-waving aren't going to carry much weight. With some practice, you'll become skilled at explaining your rationale and commanding respect for your ideas.

So, toughen up. When people ask questions or challenge your conclusions, it means you're working for an A company, instead of a B company. Having robust discussions about important topics is what well-functioning teams do. If a presentation ends quietly with a few perfunctory questions and no real discussion, that's a failure of the whole team. You need to create an environment in which challenges can be raised, real issues discussed, and the pros and cons of each decision laid on the table for open analysis. That can't happen if you're unwilling to tolerate some push back. Your presentation has served its purpose only when it has provoked a challenge.

Suppose someone challenges your results, and sure enough, you did make a mistake. Now you look like an idiot. Don't dwell on it right away. Go through your day and put some distance between you and the event. When you have some time, maybe later at home, and can look at the big picture, think it through and decide what the next correct step is. Don't blame the person who pointed out the error—that's his or her job. And don't take it personally. Everyone makes mistakes—it doesn't mean you're a flawed person; it just means you have more to learn in your position. That's okay; you will. Right now you need to focus on recovering and moving forward.

Here's a tip that works for me, and maybe it will help you, too. I say to myself, "Don't get even; get mad." If you participate in competitive sports, have you ever found yourself down a few points, and getting kind of ticked off? Taking advantage of that emotional edge can help you buckle down, focus a lot, and show a bit more grit. It comes in handy when you have to do something hard or overcome an adversity. When I screw up, I find this reaction more empowering than slinking around like a loser. It helps me perform better *after* I've recovered from feeling like a ninny.

Get Mad and Move On

Challenges can lead to conflict, another difficult area for many women. Some people thrive on conflict; they seem to get up in the morning, ready for a good tangle, and come out swinging, honking on the freeway, muscling people on the phone, hassling a stranger at the bar. Guess what—this won't surprise you—I am not that person. Conflict at work and in my personal life has always made me feel bad, and it was a long way into my career before I started to get a handle on how to use it.

If you're like me, early in your career, you'll recognize that conflict is inherent to the workplace, but you try to make it as painless and positive as possible. You work on strategies to present bad news or negative feedback to people in as gentle a way as possible. You try to avoid unnecessarily upsetting people. If you're involved in a conflict between two people, you work as a go-between, to downplay emotions, and avoid a confrontation. You become expert at building bridges, diplomacy, clarifying points of common interest, nurturing collaborative processes, seeking rational resolutions, and on and on. That's all good, but you know what? Sometimes guys just want to have a big shouting match. It's not your fault. It's not your responsibility to keep it from happening. And you shouldn't worry about it.

Because here's the deal with a lot of businessmen: Confrontation doesn't bother them that much; accordingly, it shouldn't bother *you* that much. Did anybody die? No. Many men seem to be able to have a fight, and when it's over, they move on. They're not denying it happened. It happened, and now it's over. They don't worry about it, and they're not damaged by it. They seem to be able to come out of a big blowup with their relationship intact. There's an element of trust on both sides that, even though each person was mad as hell, and they had to get their points across in a superheated screamfest, they can still get along afterward, and the company won't collapse because of it.

This can be confusing to women; it certainly was to me. When people yelled at each other, I cringed and feared that they were damaging their relationship and were saying things they would regret. All that hostility and unleashed emotion made me sick. "How are we ever going to recover from this?" I'd think. Then the next day, the fighters would be perfectly fine (if they were guys, *not* if they were women), and I'd be baffled.

For men, there's a sense that "This isn't personal: We're on the soccer field, it's a battle, but once we step off, we'll be fine." That depersonalization of the interaction is less familiar to women. It's more likely to be instilled in us that when there's an argument, it's *very* personal. Because women shy away from conflict, they've had fewer opportunities to learn how to deal with it in ways that don't threaten their relationships. They don't have those skills yet. Perhaps having more girls playing sports will improve this situation. With more girls competing with each other and staying friends—win or lose—maybe they'll worry less about someone getting her feelings hurt.

I'm reminded of one manager's creative approach to conflict resolution. He was a very serious corporate controller, not known to have a sense of humor at all. He had installed some consolidation software that the division controllers *hated*. There was considerable grumbling at our annual meeting when we prepared for budget season, so he took us out for dinner and ordered a HUGE fancy drink, full of all kinds of rums and liquors, and mixers, and fancy straws, and things sticking out the top. Holding this decorative statement over his head, he bawled out, "Does anyone still have a problem with the consolidation software?" We all raised our hands in a show of anti-corporate solidarity. "Fine," he groused. "Send this thing around," and the drink proceeded to be passed from person to person so we could take a slurp. When the drink came back to him, he bawled out again, "Now, who still has a problem with the software?" There were still some hands, but more laughing, and fewer hands than before. "Okay," he said, "Send it around again." I don't remember how many trips it took or how many drinks he ordered, but I do remember in the end, we all ended up ruefully laughing, with no hands in the air. We weren't drunk—but the software fight was over, and we all had to be friends again.

Being able to move on after an argument is somewhat freeing. If conflict manifests itself in a big fight, but life can go on once it's over, it's not that scary. It's just a thing guys do; it's not that big of a deal. It helped me see that this violence wasn't irreparable and made me tougher. If men got mad and yelled at me, it wasn't that devastating because I could think, "Oh, well, he'll get over it." With most guys, once he's stopped shouting, your relationship can go right back to what it was, pre-shouting.

If competition, challenge and conflict flair up into a gigantic fight at work, I hope you won't be too upset by it. It's not as serious for guys as it might appear to you. The more you see it, live around it, and survive it, the easier it will be for you to put it behind you and move onto something more fun.

CHAPTER FIVE

Danger—Falling Coconuts

INTERACTIONS BETWEEN MEN AND WOMEN at work can be complicated because both genders tend to fall back on the ways in which they're accustomed to interacting *outside* the workplace. Old habits die hard, even when we're consciously aware that our colleagues are not our wives, sisters, sons, etc. Here are some specific pitfalls that executive women must watch out for.

Sit Down and Shut Up

Far and away, the most common mistake I see women making around men is talking too much. Assume that every moment you speak will be multiplied in a man's mind by two or three. If you speak in a meeting as much as the guys do, their impression will be that you dominated the discussion. Most guys are terrible listeners anyway, but they especially don't like listening to a woman, *particularly* if she gets going on a diatribe or a lecture. It's a rare guy who will listen to you with attention and patience. If you encounter one, either he'll turn out to be your dad, or you should marry him immediately.

I'm Talking—No, *I'm* Talking

In the work environment, there's limited airtime, and guys compete to take up most of it. In their minds, dominating the airwaves is a good way to prove their superiority. If someone's listening to you, it automatically puts him in an inferior position. Guys think no one actually chooses to be silent; they assume a guy's who's not talking is either over-powered or can't think of anything to say.

A meeting, especially a big one, can be a real pressure cooker in that kind of environment. Guys get quite wound up about this and spend an enormous amount of energy after meetings, either recanting at length the clever things they said, or complaining how somebody else went "on and on" and didn't have anything to say. If they attend a meeting in which they didn't talk much, they'll describe it as "boring" and a "waste of time."

Never fear, girlfriend, all this plays into your hands perfectly. First, most women are naturally good listeners and don't chafe at the idea of listening to other people talk for hours on end. That's good because you're going to spend much of your career listening, and most of it listening to men.

Learn to Listen

If you're not naturally a good listener, you *must* develop that skill. Pay attention when someone is talking, especially if you're the only listener. What's he saying? Put aside your own thoughts and opinions for a minute and really listen to him. Stop trying to jump in and compete for airtime. Pay him the courtesy of an opportunity to express his views, explain something, complain, or maybe even compliment you. Give him your undivided attention:

Turn off your phone, hold your calls, shut the door. Use your eyes and face to show him you're really listening with open ears and an open mind.

This is such a rare experience for him it may make a profound impression on him. Don't be surprised if he brings up this experience years later with admiration and gratitude. I've found "quiet" guys can be extremely talkative in private, and they appreciate an opportunity to express themselves without having to fight for airtime.

What's He Really Saying?

Now, listen even harder. Listen to what he's telling you on a deeper level. Ask yourself why he's saying this to you, and why now? Is he trying to impress you? Is he asking for your support? Is he trying to learn something from you? Is he just killing time until his next meeting starts? Look at him and study his face. Watch his eyes. Is he being truthful? Is he upset about something that he's having trouble talking about? Is he mad at you and hiding it?

Participate in the communication: Nod if you agree, smile if he cracks a joke, let your body react naturally as you process what he's saying, cock your head if you're musing or confused. A guy gets off on talking to a woman who's genuinely listening to him. Put everything you've got into active listening. He'll notice, he'll appreciate it, and he'll remember.

Listening Brings Knowledge

Here's the payoff. Listening arms you with incredibly valuable information. Think of how much you learn when you listen to others. You learn what their thoughts are, what they consider important, their prejudices, personality, fears and insecurities. You may discover they're mean and arrogant, or they're generous and care about others. You may learn about their personal situation, political views, religion and upbringing. You've gained this knowledge, and they haven't learned anything about you except that you listen well.

Be aware that guys are often more comfortable confiding in women than they are in other guys. They don't see you as competition, so several layers of reserve are eliminated. They're also less likely to see you as threatening or intimidating, or any of the other suspicions that keep people from openly talking to each other.

Listening Brings Respect

Surprisingly, after talking to you for a while, guys often assume they know more about you than they do. Of course, they can make the obvious observation—that you're a good listener. But because you've demonstrated an unusual level of respect, they'll also identify you as courteous and thoughtful. They may attribute other characteristics to you as well, which might be unfounded but flattering nonetheless. For instance, they may think you're smarter than most women. They won't ever think you're very smart (sorry), but they may be willing to ascribe some level of intelligence to you since at least you're smart enough to listen to them.

They may privately describe you to someone else in ways that would totally surprise you. They may remark on your level of experience and knowledge. They may comment on how valuable your input was, and how rewarding it was to speak with you. Finally, they may recommend that others speak to you too.

And other people will act on that recommendation. Soon, more and more people will want to spend time with you. Your phone starts to ring more frequently. Your email box is piling up. You begin to suffer from an overload of information. You may learn more about other people's opinions, allegiances, and conflicts than you ever thought possible. Unfortunately, guys aren't very discreet, so you may learn more than you'd like about various political intrigues, personnel issues, and indiscretions.

Listening Builds Relationships

Building relationships with your male colleagues is extremely important and an area that executive women don't always develop as they should. Become part of the network. Call guys on the phone to pass along useful, non-confidential information. Sometimes just call to check in. Guys actually do this. Stop by their offices. It reminds them you exist and may uncover an opportunity for you to work together. Use your contacts—call people up, ask questions. They'll return your calls, they'll call you to tell you about corporate developments, and they want to know what you know. They'll take you in, but you have to be a participant—not an on-looker.

I used to tell my staff, "When someone calls to say they're just calling to give you a 'heads-up,' duck! It's invariably bad." There's some truth to that, but you'd rather get the 'heads-up' call than not have your phone ring.

As guys get to know you, they'll want to talk to you in private and in public. They'll want other guys to know they know you and be seen with you. They'll catch you in the hallway and ask you along to meetings, they'll ask you to join the group at the bar or the ballpark, and they'll invite you on important trips. Don't worry about being the only woman. They already know you're different, and they think that's cool.

Knowledge Is Power

Warning: Knowledge is power, and you've just been given a boatload of it. Be very careful how you use it. Any use you make of what you now know should be moral and to the company's benefit, not for your personal gain. Don't use your knowledge to hurt, damage, or torture people. It's up to you to use your power wisely and kindly.

And don't betray confidences. That's a terrible, mean thing to do to someone. Even if your confidant didn't specifically ask you to keep something secret, if your intuition tells you the information was probably given in confidence, respect that. Always err on the side of silence. Most people are awful at keeping secrets. Be the exception.

This knowledge can protect you and your staff (and maybe even your boss) from nasty office politics. Since you're aware of relationships, both formal and informal, you can predict and sway the outcome of politicized events. You can keep someone from being unfairly blamed or cast in an unfavorable light if you know there exist preconceived prejudices against him or her. As your career progresses, you'll become more adept at navigating office politics and softening its negative impact because you can see ahead and act quickly to stop detrimental incidents.

What a turnabout this is. Far from being the ostracized woman, the poor soul who's left out of the Men's room, you're now in the thick of everything. You know more about everyone in the group than they know about each other, or about you. You know more up and down the organizational chart than anyone at your level. You know who's being groomed, who's in trouble, who's leaving and why, and where everyone is likely to be in a year's time. All by listening. Who's feeling sorry for the little woman now?

How Do You Get Anything Done?

You can imagine this can get out of hand. You can't spend all your time listening to people talk. You're paid for other activities as well, and your new listening self will turn out to be better at those activities than you were before.

Think what a remarkable position you're in. You've developed a bird's-eye view of the whole organization allowing you to see which parts are functional and which need serious help. You can also put fragments of information together to form solutions since you know who can work together and who's more likely to kill each other.

Have you ever worked with a consultant who developed a phenomenal understanding of the organization in a short period of time simply by asking questions and listening to people? Now you're that consultant, but you get to stay with the company, instead of constantly moving onto the next assignment.

Control Your Schedule

Now, you have to keep from spending all your time with people who come see you. This can be a real trap in your progressing career. Be honest with people who stop by; if this is a busy time, let them know. Don't pretend to have time and then display poor listening behavior by being distracted and frazzled. It comes off as disinterested and rude instead of just busy. If you must turn someone away, communicate your regret (after all, he or she may have something important to tell you) and schedule another time to get together.

A short period of time is better than no time. If you have five minutes, that's enough time for a good quality conversation. Let them know you only have five minutes, then really listen. When five minutes are up, assert yourself politely, and say goodbye.

You need some tricks for stopping a discussion, a monologue, or a rant. Practice different tactics: Look at your watch, stand up, stretch, smile, say politely that you're sorry but you've got to move onto something else. Learn what works for you. Be regretful because you are. If you're really a good listener, you're interested in what he has to say. But you have other responsibilities, too.

Be honest. Don't pretend to have another meeting when you don't. Don't have your assistant interrupt you with some phony emergency. Just say you've got work to do, and you have to earn your keep. Guys understand this. Although they may act as though they're the most important people on earth, they know you have a job to do.

If someone is monopolizing your time, deliberately develop a plan to deal with him. Discourage his drop-in visits, and set specific times to see him. Schedule those times far enough out in the future that there will be something important to discuss. Again, be regretful but clear. And don't feel guilty; after all he's had a lot of your time already. Other people need you. Don't be a patsy and let someone take up all your time.

Step Back from the Brink

What if someone starts coming to see you all the time and begins treating you like his therapist? Is he starting to talk to you more about his personal life than about work issues? Does he seek your counsel about his wife and their relationship? Is their relationship bad? Wake up, girl! This is dangerous territory. First, he may be on the verge of falling in love with you. That's a disaster and can't happen. Second, people are horrifically observant of this behavior and love to spread dreadful rumors about it. Make sure you give them no fuel for that fire. Don't spend an inordinate amount of time behind closed doors with someone. Don't treat one guy differently than you do the others. Stop this problem guy in his tracks.

He Doesn't Think You're Very Smart

Most guys don't think women are very smart. No matter how many degrees, diplomas, Mensa memberships, or Phi Beta Kappa keys you wave around, he probably won't be impressed. His only observation will be that you're full of yourself. On the other hand, outside of academia, no one really cares how smart you are. Most business people admire shrewdness, a good memory, or some level of glibness, but brain power doesn't particularly appeal to them. They can't relate to fine reasoning, significant mental capacity, or a facility with complex formulas and concepts. Too much braininess makes them uncomfortable, and they'd rather point out how dumb "smart" people are.

A guy is sometimes willing to admit that another guy is pretty smart—usually when they're in agreement about an issue. But he won't attribute this characteristic to you. It's just not part of his consciousness. He probably didn't think his mom was very smart; he knows his wife isn't.

Don't Outsmart Him

It's okay to know something he doesn't, though I wouldn't be show-offy about it. But don't point out flaws in his reasoning or that an action he just took was absurd. Don't lord knowledge, skills, or intellect over him. You'll just make him mad. If you have to point out a mistake, do so gracefully and find a way for him to save face. Sometimes the best approach is to ask a series of leading (and honest) questions that attempt to follow his thought process. Either you'll discover that what he did was sensible and you just didn't understand it, or you'll both discover he made an error in logic. After all, he doesn't want a mistake to go forward, and he'll be grateful you caught it. He doesn't see you as competition, so it doesn't mean much if you point out a mistake. If his error is caught by another guy, he might get defensive and try to justify some bone-headed move. But he can take some correction from you.

The Good News

You have a wonderful opportunity here. First, you're smarter than he thinks. No matter how dumb you are, girlfriend, he thinks you're dumber. But he's willing to pick your brain and take input from you. He'll get more comfortable doing this as he learns that you give great advice, can write reasonably well, know more than you share, understand discounted cash flows, have figured out the security system, and can carry a tune. You're not smart, but you're *useful.* And you, my smart little cookie, have now got an ally.

Who cares if he doesn't think you're smart? The trick is to get him to listen to you. As long as you've found a way to get him to seek your counsel and pay attention to what you say, that's good enough—in fact, it's huge. It means you're on your way!

But Don't Be Dumb

Now you're in this powerful spot, don't blow it. Too often I've seen women get to a strong position, only to give it up. We're accustomed to interacting with men in certain ways, and it's difficult to break those habits. Now that you have his respect, treasure it. Don't undermine what you've accomplished by relaxing and falling into stereotypical behavior just because he's a guy. Avoid falling into the following six traps:

Trap #1: Don't Let Him Turn You into His Wife

He probably mostly likes his wife. And now he mostly likes you. But he's accustomed to behaving around his wife in a certain way. And, heck, you're both women, so that's probably how he should behave around you, right? No. Dead wrong. Don't go there. If he starts getting cute with you, cut it off. If he starts pretending he's just a big buffoon, but of course you love him anyway, you need to draw back and re-establish the relationship on a more professional level.

Here are the danger signs of male executives getting too comfortable with their female employees: chatting unreservedly about personal stuff, asking her opinion about his clothes or appearance, flirting, trying to turn her into his personal cheerleader, acting like a little boy, denying his importance or power by pretending to plead for something. Ick. Step back from that ledge. Turn the conversation back to a work topic, or look at your watch and say you better get to work. Sometimes just walking out is good enough. He needs to respect you as a professional, take you seriously, and be aware of your power. And you do too.

Trap #2: Don't Let Him Turn You into His Mother

He might love his mother, but that's likely to be a complex relationship. Don't let him attribute qualities to you that many boys see in their mother: She nags, she's bossy, she puts him down. He doesn't like being belittled. Because you're a woman, however, he may think you're naturally going to behave like his mother. He'll be watching for "motherly" behavior and may accuse you of this even when you're not guilty of it. Be careful not to engage in behaviors that are reminiscent of mothers: taking care of him, making sure he has lunch or food, reminding him of things he should have remembered himself, nagging, being overly sympathetic no matter what dumb bunny thing he's done, etc.

Trap #3: Don't Let Him Turn You into His Secretary

These are just variations on the themes above, but don't let him confuse the roles of the women who work around him. If you and his administrative assistant are stumbling over each other because he has asked you to make appointments and phone calls for him, make sure you clarify who is to do what, and don't vary from what's agreed. Usually you and the admin can sort this out between you and just let him know what you've agreed.

Trap #4: Don't Treat Him Like a Baby

If your boss is the CEO, you may notice a phenomenon that was described to me by a clever investor relations professional—"the infantilization of the CEO." Perhaps because this is the era of the rock-star CEO, senior management teams seem to unconsciously collude to treat the CEO as though he's a baby whom everyone needs to pamper and coddle. Once it was pointed out to me, I saw it a lot. And some CEOs even encourage it. The illusion is that the rest of the team is made up of Clydesdale work horses, built to take the hard blows, but the CEO is some kind of delicate thoroughbred who can be easily damaged by typical corporate ups and downs. Bad news is kept from him, information is presented in ways to minimize distress, there's considerable preoccupation with his physical comfort—his office, his coffee; every little whim is treated as though it's of corporate importance. You need to step back from this kind of nonsense, and remind your peers this guy's supposed to be the toughest of them all.

Trap #5: Don't Go Shopping with the Spouses

When spouses are invited to company meetings, I've sometimes seen the junior female employees head off with the spouses to their "women's event." I wouldn't do this. This seems very wrong to me. Sorry, if you want to go to that art show or whatever, go on your own time. If there's a general mix of executives and spouses at all events, that's one thing, but in my experience, they split up. And when they do, you want to be on the *executive* side.

Don't worry about speaking up if there's an unspoken implication that you'll go hang with the wives because you're a woman. Differentiate yourself by saying openly that you want to participate in the executive activity. Guys will appreciate your clarity. They often aren't sure what you prefer, and they assume that you'd rather be with your own kind, as defined by your gender.

Trap #6: Don't Stay Home

I've been fortunate to work for tennis-playing companies instead of golf-playing companies, and I play tennis, so I could hold my own when it came time for recreation. If you don't play your company's sport and you're serious about the organization, consider picking it up. Get a few lessons and see if you can get good enough to participate. If not, ask if you can just tag along. If you're a pleasant person, the guys will be delighted to have you there. Sometimes they think you wouldn't be interested if you don't play. Disabuse them of that dumb assumption—you're very interested.

I'm hoping your company's sport is something civilized. If it's hunting, off-roading, or drinking, you can give it a pass. Since lots of guys don't like those activities either, maybe you can suggest an alternative. I have to ask, though, if that's the case, what *are* you doing in that company? And you don't have to go to strip clubs either, my friend.

For some reason, it's become popular to say joyfully that women can be successful at business *without* learning to play golf! Is learning to play golf such a terrible thing? It sounds fun to me, and don't you want to spend time with the men you work with? If you don't, may I respectfully suggest you move to a company run by people with whom you do want to spend time? Remember, you don't have to be good at sports. You just have to be there. In fact, it's better if you're not good. Men *hate* being beaten by a girl.

CHAPTER SIX

Touchy Subjects

THE PREVIOUS CHAPTER DISCUSSED potential pitfalls that executive women should avoid. This chapter will address giant, dangerous, career-ending mistakes that you must not commit at all costs. Here you will learn how to socialize with the men you work with, how to behave after hours, and how to handle sex at work. This chapter is pretty explicit and direct—I don't want to offend you, but I want to be clear. These are areas where I have seen women ruin their careers, and yet career advice books and mentors often avoid discussing them. So, let's you and I talk about them.

After Hours

Okay, let's get down to the nitty-gritty. What goes down after hours when you're the only girl in a bunch of guys? Start with this: Everything that happens after hours, you control. From the moment the venue is selected, the activities are planned, and the participants sorted out, you decide whether or not to attend, what you wear, and how you behave—these choices are up to you, and they dictate what happens next.

Like to Get to Know You

These events are fun and useful, so be sure to attend. Companies sponsor after-hours events for business reasons—they're not just to pass the time or to keep you out of your hotel room for an evening. They're supposed to help build strong teams or establish connections between departments, or just to say 'thank you.' Take advantage of them; don't hole up in your hotel room like you're a leper or afraid of men. You're not! You like men—you work with them every day.

Company events offer a terrific opportunity to get to know some of the guys who are too shy to interact with you at work, may be afraid of you, or have a preconceived notion about you. Now you can break through those barriers and establish a relationship. Be yourself. Have a beer. Tell a joke. Kid around a little. Let the guys get to know you. You're usually in a listening mode at work—now you can turn on and sparkle.

If you don't know someone, introduce yourself. If someone is standing alone, include him in your conversation. Tread lightly because you don't want to overwhelm or intimidate him, but be brave. If he doesn't know the others, introduce him. Don't forget those colleagues you interact with frequently. If you have a relationship with a guy, acknowledge him. Don't ignore him when you're in a larger group—you'll hurt his feelings. Don't stand forlornly by yourself. Don't make a guy approach you to get a conversation started; it will feel like a pickup to him, and he'll try to avoid that.

Be confident of your role in this situation. Most men enjoy having a woman around in social situations; it gives them an excuse to talk about something other than work, it reminds them of home and family, and it adds some pizzazz to an environment that might otherwise be kind of dull.

The Spark of the Party

At the beginning of your career, *you* might be more comfortable in these situations than the men are. You're likely to have superior social skills and more experience with how to behave at a nice restaurant or a cocktail party than they do. Later, as you rise in the organization, your male colleagues will be more accustomed to these quasi-social occasions and will be able to interact in a more relaxed way. But young businessmen are sometimes so anxious they might say something wrong that they hardly say anything. Many times, I've encountered a group of young male work colleagues standing around uncomfortably, clinging to a sweaty beer, because they don't know how to relate to their colleagues outside of work. Here is a chance for you to shine and help put them at ease. You can show them that these occasions aren't life or death professionally.

Get a conversation going. Recant any funny thing that happened to you on the way over to the event. Mention a recent news item. Is there a game on TV? Ask who's winning. Keep abreast of major sports news so you can converse. If sports are being discussed, you'll want to participate. You don't have to know very much to ask questions or make a comment or two. If you don't know something, ask. Men don't expect women to know much about sports, and they're happy to have a conversation in which they can show off.

Make it short and zippy, and make it inclusive. Don't buttonhole somebody and start peppering him with personal questions in an attempt to "get to know him." Ask questions of the general group: Where are people staying? Have you been to the pool? Were you guys swimmers in high school? If people start side conversations once things are underway—that's great. You don't want to be the center of attention, but you may have to act as a catalyst.

Down with Dull

Try to develop the discussion into something meaningful and memorable. Don't have the same old tired conversations that everyone has in those situations: when did you get here, how was your flight, when are you going back, are you enjoying the conference... Eiyeiyei! Try to learn something; practice active listening; attempt some genuine communication.

Don't avoid "dangerous topics." I'm sick of people saying we shouldn't talk about politics, religion or the real news. You talk about these things among family and friends, don't you? They're interesting topics, and it's possible to talk about them in a non-threatening, non-polarizing way. Just leave room for people who have different views. Listen hard. Was this guy raised Mormon? Does this guy share his dad's political viewpoint? Be non-judgmental. Ask genuine questions. Point out the legitimacy of the opposite view. You don't have to share your personal position, but feel free to if you want. Most guys are comfortable stating their political views—why shouldn't you?

These occasions can be tons of fun. Act as though there's no place else you'd rather be. Take some risks. If the guys are acting stuffy, do something they would consider nutty. Play some pinball, go to the top floor to look out, run next door for better snacks. Tease the bartender. Make a drawing of something you're explaining. Order a weird drink. Don't push too hard, but I'm sure if you put your imagination to work and let go of some inhibitions, you can come up with some ideas. Just don't make it all about you and suck all the oxygen out of the room.

Dress Code

Do dress like yourself. If it's an informal event, you should choose clothes that reflect your personality. If you're a Cubs fan, wear a Cubbies hat (expect some well-deserved ribbing). If you're a jeans gal, wear jeans. If you like cowboy boots, wear 'em. It doesn't hurt to wear something they can comment on and kid you about. At least it gives them something to talk about.

But don't give them something that's going to keep them awake at night. Don't dress provocatively. This is a work occasion, not a fashion show or a date. The guys you work with don't want to see you as sexy—they don't want the burden of being attracted to you. They find it distracting and would rather not have to deal with that. In my experience, men invariably notice if women wear revealing clothing and respond to that. Don't do tight, short, low-cut, skimpy, or hot.

After one all-day meeting, I met the guys in the bar. The conversation was well underway when one of my female colleagues showed up in a low-cut blouse that featured her ample bosom. We were a bit taken aback as there hadn't been any previous indication she was *that* sort of girl. Even I was struck speechless. After she'd wandered off a bit awkwardly, one of the guys said quietly to her back, "Put some clothes on!" And another murmured, "Yeah, jeez." I suspect she had no idea how uncomfortable she'd made them. I recognize this is difficult, ladies. We're accustomed to using our charms to entice and attract men. Work situations are different. You're not looking to propagate the human race, just maybe a little relationship-building and some fun.

Stay in Control

Don't be loud, and don't get drunk. Although you'll want to relax a little, don't forget that this is a work event and you have a professional reputation to protect. Keep track of how many drinks you've had and switch to non-alcoholic ones if you start to feel tipsy. I find it hard sometimes to get much food when I'm socializing; be careful about drinking on an empty stomach.

Be aware of your surroundings. Have you gotten engrossed in a conversation with someone and suddenly realize everyone else has left? Go home. Have you had too much to drink? Go home. Have you run out of things to talk about? Go home. Don't let yourself get into vulnerable situations—that's when very bad things can happen that you'll deeply regret later.

Do stay with the group. If one of the guys suggests you go off and do something different, decline politely. The event has been sponsored in order for you to interact with the group, not to facilitate a date with a colleague.

A Quiz

Female executives sometimes make mistakes during after-hours events. How about a quiz here to see how you're assimilating the advice in this book? Is the following the right or wrong way to attend a mostly-male after-hours company event?

- Come late, or not at all, because you have to "work."
- Ignore the guys and talk only to other women.
- Stand around talking soberly about company business.
- Never tell a joke, and loudly announce that you know nothing about sports.

If you answered "right" to any of these, go back to the beginning of the book and start over.

One-on-One: Danger Zones

One-on-one meetings can be more difficult and more dangerous. In general, when you're a junior employee, don't meet one-on-one with a male colleague outside work. Have your meetings at work, in your office, his office, or a conference room. However, don't have endless meetings with the same guy behind closed doors; you'll start a rumor.

Lunch, Drinks, and Dinner

Lunch outside the office is fine, but I wouldn't make a habit of always eating with the same guy. That's just fodder for the gossips and probably gets old for both of you. Make sure it's in a public place and doesn't go on too long.

Drinks are okay if there's a delicate topic that needs to be discussed outside the office without the interruptions of phone calls and other meetings. At more senior levels, personnel issues, strategic moves, ideas about mergers and acquisitions, brainstorming about financing, career decisions—these are subjects that can be discussed over a drink. I tend to drink lemonade at those meetings because I don't want to get fuzzy, but if you feel like having a drink, cheers! Just don't forget what Dorothy Parker said: "I like to have a martini, two at the very most. After three I'm under the table, after four I'm under the host!"

Drinks and dinner one-on-one is dangerous territory. If you're not traveling and aren't at a senior level, avoid this. They're just too much like a date and will confuse both of you. See if you can convert it into just drinks. You may have to think quickly to determine if he's asking you out, or if he thought it was a fine idea to have drinks and dinner to talk something over. You can groom your response accordingly. Keep in mind he may not be sure which it is either. There may be exceptions; if his wife's out of town, and he's a bit lonely always eating alone, you can help him out. But make sure your attitude is business-like.

If you want to decline entirely, do so politely—you don't have to say why. Just say you'd rather not. It's flattering that he thought you were interesting enough to spend more time with. Be appreciative of that and sensitive to his feelings. Be straightforward. Don't make up some phony excuse or say you're busy. He won't know where to go with that.

A Girl Can Be a Guy's Best Friend

If you've worked with someone for a long time and would trust him implicitly, you can have drinks and dinner with him, but be ever vigilant for a change in his attitude. If his reserve starts to break down, be ready to cut that off. Remember, if he's a good guy, he doesn't really want to get involved with you—he might just be a little lonely, or jet-lagged, or mad at his girlfriend. Don't let him make a mistake. If you save him from that, he'll know what happened, and he'll always be grateful.

At more senior levels, one-on-one dinners are acceptable, if there's a specific topic to be discussed and a business reason for the event. Sometimes for personnel or political issues, meetings need to take place off-site, and dinner meetings can be a gracious way to be a host or a guest. But, even at this level, don't get sloppy and get into trouble.

When you're traveling with someone, dinner meetings are harder to avoid. Think ahead; don't get caught unawares. See if you can get someone else to come along to dinner, and keep it snappy. Don't linger, and don't let the dynamic of the encounter change.

Who Pays?

If it's a business event, and business was genuinely discussed, the senior person or the finance person should pick up the tab. Otherwise, go dutch. If he insists on paying, make sure you say that next time you'll pay, and do it. Don't let him get in the habit of paying for you. Eventually, he may expect something in return. This only applies to work colleagues. If he's a vendor, and you're a customer, it's customary for him to pay, and there's no implied sexual credit that's due.

Sex at Work

Don't have sex with people you work with. I say this clearly and bluntly because it's important. When you're in a business setting, you must behave in a businesslike way to participate productively in company activities, and that doesn't include having sex. If you want to be taken seriously as a businesswoman, you can't intermingle your love life and work life. You'll be judged very harshly if you bring sex into the workplace. You'll also irreparably spoil a presumably important work relationship. It's extremely distracting to you and your co-workers and not an effective use of your company's time, to say the least. It's not funny or cute. It's deadly serious and can ruin your career. If it becomes known (and assume that it will), I would say it's *the* most damaging thing you can do to your career at that company, besides stealing. Don't do it. Ever.

Are There Exceptions?

Oh, I knew you'd want to talk about exceptions. Sigh. Okay, suppose you've met the love of your life, and of course, finding a soul mate *is* more important than your career. However, your "soul mate" *cannot* be anyone with whom you have a line relationship, that is, someone to whom you report or who reports to you, no matter how many levels there are between you. Sorry, those individuals are completely off-limits, no matter how "soul mate-ish" they may look. If your boyfriend is your subordinate, you could be accused of sexual harassment, and your company simply can't run that risk. It's too dangerous and could be very expensive. And, vice versa, your boyfriend better be smart enough to realize he can't sleep with you if he's higher than you are in the reporting structure. After all, you don't want to have sex with a fool.

What if it's someone in a different department, and you recognize that you're playing with *fire*—is there any reasonable way to handle it?

First rule: Tell NO ONE. People simply are incapable of keeping this kind of gossip secret. Trust NO ONE, and make sure your boyfriend understands that. If he's your soul mate, he should get it.

Second rule: Get out. You better decide pretty quickly who's going to leave the company because news of your relationship *will* leak, and it's better for you if it leaks *after* one of you has left. Even then, don't be surprised at how betrayed and angry your manager and co-workers may feel when it comes out, even if it's after one or both of you are gone.

I've heard people say that employees become more loyal to a company if their paramour is also employed there. I've observed just the opposite. Almost always, one half of the couple will leave to get out of an uncomfortable situation, and it's almost always the woman, because the man's career is seen as more important. Moving fast, for a bad reason, can damage your career because it usually results in taking a less-than-ideal job. In addition, couples often want to dissipate risk. If something goes wrong at the company, they don't want to have all their eggs in one basket. So, be very shrewd when you consider your options.

Where Are Those Skeptical Spectacles?

But let's be honest here: You've met the love of your life, and he just happens to work at your company? Come on. What are the chances? It's more probable that you're spending lots of time at work, and you've stumbled onto a person who's likeable and charming, but he's not the only fish in the sea. Is it really worth sacrificing all the great work you've done at that company to build your reputation, skill set, and knowledge base for some guy?

Speaking of probability, how many people live in your town? Does the population exceed the number of company employees? If yes, then your soul mate is more likely to work *outside* your company. Ever heard of Match.com? eHarmony? Now your chances get even better. I acknowledge there are special cases, if you live in a one-company town, or if you're working abroad, but I would still strongly encourage a skeptical view and ensure you exhaust *all* other options before you're tempted by a co-worker.

Sex Is Everywhere

Despite my sound advice, office romances flourish, at every level of the organization. Co-workers have affairs, executives sleep with their assistants, managers date, and on and on. When I look back, I'm surprised by how much sex I've encountered at work. And yet nobody talks about it! If someone had told me when I took my first job how big a role sex would play in corporate America, I wouldn't have believed it, but it might have prevented me from being as shocked. Let's make you better prepared.

We already know *you* won't be one of the people carrying on an affair at work, but suppose you find yourself working with some lovebirds. Here are some tips to survive this awkward situation.

- *Maintain a professional attitude.* Don't gossip about the couple or the affair. Don't acknowledge it at all unless one of the players reports to you. Put thoughts of the issue out of your mind when you interact with those involved to avoid getting distracted or sucked into a conversation you don't want to have. If one of the actors broaches the topic with you directly, you can say, "That's your business, and not mine." Make it clear this topic is off-limits.
- *Set boundaries.* If one of the people reports to you, it's much harder. If the couple is behaving in an overtly sexual way at work, you have to intervene. It's wrong for that distracting behavior to be on display in front of other employees. Work with the human resources department to confront your

employee and give very specific directions about what's acceptable behavior and what's not. For example, "You're not allowed to touch each other." "You must maintain a distance of three feet between you on company property." "You're not allowed to kiss on company property, even in your car." Emphasize that the affair is not against company policy, but the distracting behavior during work hours is.

- *Take her aside.* If you have a mentoring relationship with either party, I would take the opportunity to counsel against an office romance and urge discretion and eventual departure from the company, just as I have for you. Explain how damaging office flings are to a career, particularly for women.

Even at the Executive Level

What if you're a senior manager, or board member, and you become aware of an office romance at the executive level? Ah, now we'll see out what you're made of. Are you going to shirk your responsibilities, or are you brave enough to handle this tricky situation? You're probably not in this situation today, but it's worth thinking about so you can be ready if you ever are. The first consideration is the company and the shareholders. Be aware there's terrible liability connected with sex in the workplace. No matter how much you think the company won't get sued, if it does, it will probably settle out of court, and it will be *very* expensive. And don't try to tell me the executive got trapped by some lower-level employee. It doesn't work that way; at least the law won't see it that way. Therefore, no matter how much you like the exec, you have no choice. He or she must go—as fast as possible. This no-tolerance approach will send a powerful message, to potential predators to leave your employees alone, and to your employees that you're on their side and they won't be harassed while they work at your company.

Three More Reasons Sex at Work Is Bad

1. *Sex distorts the power structure of an organization.*
   Power is divided up according to the organizational chart which has been carefully designed to maintain division of labor, segregation of responsibilities, good internal controls, and good governance. Employees who establish a separate intimate relationship create alliances across the organization that distort this careful structure. If the head of quality assurance starts sleeping with one of the manufacturing guys, your quality controls have been compromised, and that should worry you.

2. *You will pay more than he does.*
   I was involved with a company where two top executives suddenly began sleeping together (or it appeared sudden to me since one of them was still married). I was surprised how quickly news spread, how distressing this was to the employees, and how poorly it was perceived. The employees recognized that it presented a definite risk to the company and to their employment. News also traveled to our collaborators, and I was privy to their reaction and snide comments. I was surprised by how irritated they were at this distraction and, *in particular,* how critical they were of the woman, even though she wasn't the married one. Their anger was mostly directed at her, their judgment was harsh, and their comments were crude. So take note, little sister, it's *not* an even playing field, and you need to stay out of this kind of trouble.

3. *Guys just hate a sexual woman at work.*
   I'll venture a theory that this reaction isn't just blind sexism. I think most men work pretty hard to treat women in the

workplace impartially and *not* as sexual objects. That's the way we want it, right? When a woman deliberately flaunts her sexuality, it's doubly disturbing and perhaps even makes them feel duped. First, she pretends to be a professional, and now she does *this*? There's business to be taken care of, and it's not of that nature. Guys also resent a sexual woman in the workplace because it gives her access to power they have no hope of competing with. Don't play sexual games, flirt, and tease, even in subtle ways. You may have thought it was harmless, but it can bring a lot of hate down on your head.

Sex Talk at Work

What reaction will you have when you're the only woman in the room and a group of men start making sexual comments or innuendos about another woman? This happened to me fairly regularly, even though you would think my presence would account for *something*. Maybe it did at first, but I guess the guys got used to it. It gave me a window into the behaviors or attributes they noticed. Her physique, black-and-blue marks, lip-licking, breathlessness, and open mouths were all worth commenting about. To be fair, most men are disturbed by this kind of sexual exhibition at work and would prefer not to see it at all. It's worthwhile to be hyper-vigilant about your behavior and avoid any unintended stimulation.

I had a male friend who was quite miffed when female colleagues made sexual comments about men when he was present. "What am I, a eunuch?" he grumbled. I'd sometimes wondered the same thing. Had I somehow become invisible? But, in the grand scheme of things, it isn't important, and I hope it doesn't bother you. If you stay focused, and don't worry about the few jackass comments you hear, you'll be happier and more successful. If the guys turn to you and try to compromise you by saying slyly, "And what do you think, Miss So-and-So?" don't bite. I wouldn't even give them the satisfaction of seeing your discomfort. You'll develop your own style, but being a non-confrontational person, I sometimes say, "Whatever. You guys know more about that than I do." Because it's true—and irrelevant to the business at hand. After all, you're not going to fix every chauvinist you encounter. You just want to make sure he doesn't distract *you*.

The Takeaway

My advice is to keep sex strictly out of sight, even after hours, because this is *the* most dangerous area for a girl working with guys. Many mistakes are made here—terrible, career-busting mistakes—and there can be scary moments when you get confused and feel vulnerable. Stay out of this danger zone!

CHAPTER SEVEN

Guys, Guys, Guys

THE PREVIOUS FEW CHAPTERS described situations in which you're likely to interact with guys. Now let's consider some different types of guys, from Good Guys to Super Bad Guys, from gentlemen to bullies, liars and predators. We'll take a close look at sexual harassment to ensure that you know how to deal with a jerk. I dream of a time when women no longer have to worry about being harassed in the corporate world, but for now, that is still a dream.

The Big Guy

Who is the biggest of them all? Your boss. He'll have the most significant impact on your daily work life and can have a tremendous influence on your career. I'm assuming here that your boss is a guy, because in male-dominated corporations, he probably is.

A Little More Respect

Consider this tale from early in my career: I was helping my boss load his car for an important meeting in New York when I noticed he was packing some large binders that belonged to one of his subordinates. This was before laptops, and I tell you, sometimes we carried some very heavy material.

"Aren't those Todd's binders?" I asked surprised

"Yeah," my boss drawled irritably. And then he looked directly at me and said, "Jennifer, don't ever ask your boss to carry your stuff for you." What surprised me was that he had agreed to carry them! But he was clearly mad about it.

Start building your relationship on respect. This guy is your superior in the organization, so acknowledge his position and authority over you. Your job is to do what he tells you to do (within limits, obviously) and to support him. His success is your success, and you want to do everything in your power to make him successful. Sometimes it's easier said than done.

Bosses come in all colors and stripes: Some are excellent, others are terrible, but most are a blend of good and bad. Try to focus on his strengths and learn as much as you can from each boss. Sometimes all you'll learn is how to handle a wing nut, but that's beneficial, too. You always want to be looking for ways to work well with him and never at cross-purposes.

A Little Less Criticism and a Little More Obedience

To start with the obvious, don't talk badly about your boss (unless you're writing a book!). I'm surprised how frequently I hear subordinates criticizing and cutting down their managers. What a negative attitude! And how helpful are these employees to their boss or their company? Not very, I suspect. If you have so little regard for your boss that you have to undercut him all the time, you probably shouldn't be working for him.

Try to think honestly about his strengths and weaknesses, rather than being excessively critical. Think carefully about what his reasonable options were in each situation before you judge his actions. Sometimes it's easy to throw stones mindlessly. If you devote more mental effort to it, you may discover that you wouldn't have done anything differently, had you been in his shoes.

Do what he tells you to do. Again, this sounds simple, but surprisingly, employees sometimes forget this important part of their jobs. Bosses are in charge; they call the shots. If you don't do what they tell you to do, you can expect to receive a pretty negative performance appraisal. No surprise there. That's how organizations work.

Now, this doesn't mean blindly and stupidly doing what you're told, as though you don't have a brain in your head. Your boss needs you to do what he tells you to, but he also needs your intelligent input and feedback. Most bosses recognize this and really want your participation in determining how work should be completed and what your goals should be.

A Lot More Time

Most bosses don't pay enough attention to their staff members. Of course, that won't be you after you've studied the section on managing! But average business people are often too focused on their own work and careers to understand how important their staff members are to their success. You may need to be assertive to get the attention and care you need from your manager.

As you spend more time with your boss, working on your common interests, he'll become more comfortable with you and will increase the amount of time he spends with you. After a few years of working together, solving problems, and having successes, you'll have a great partnership, built on mutual respect and common experience. You're striving for that ideal from the first day. Working well with your boss can be a source of great satisfaction in your work life.

A Lot More Help

Sometimes your boss will be unclear about your job responsibilities, so don't be surprised if you have to do a little explaining. Most often, a boss underestimates how much you can help him, if you're a woman and he's a man. He's not accustomed to getting help, critical input, or real information from women, and he may not automatically seek you out. If your boss is ignoring you, you have to intervene (in a nice way) in order for him to benefit from your assistance and contributions.

You may need to set up routine meetings with him, if he doesn't seem to understand how to use you. Ask how you can help, tell him you want to contribute, and make suggestions about what you could do to make his life easier and improve the department's performance. Set up tasks and goals together you can work on and report back on. This may be a bit awkward at the beginning until he starts to see how you can help him. But, usually, once you get a rhythm going, he'll start thinking of projects on his own he'd like your help with. You'd think 100 percent of your work would come from your boss, but in my experience, bosses are often too distant from their employees and don't have a clear picture as to what they're doing or should be working on. Those aren't very good bosses, but good bosses are hard to find.

The Good, the Bad, and the Ugly

With regards to performance appraisals, you may need to show considerable initiative to elicit important feedback. When the two of you are reviewing your progress on a particular project, ask how he thought you did and if you could have done something better. It's easier for him to give you feedback in context with a specific example in mind and without the emotional pressure that comes with a formal performance appraisal. Be nice to your boss. You need his feedback; make it easy for him to give it to you. Bosses are often terribly afraid of hurting their female subordinates, particularly if they fear there might be tears. You'll have to make it safe for him to tell you what you need to know to grow and improve.

Here's a tip for you in case you do begin to get emotional while you're having a conversation with your manager, and if in fact, he *has* hurt your feelings. Go get a notepad, and take some notes. Writing down his observations will give you time to think about what he's saying, and you can rephrase them in an objective tone to get the most benefit out of the feedback. If he's dishing out some comments that have some sting to them, you can note down the gist of what he's trying to tell you and take the lash out of it. This will help you control your emotions and not overreact. Life goes on.

Don't Be a "Yes-Woman," But Let Him Drive

Beware of the boss who says your job is to make him "look good," as though you were his hairdresser. Wrong. Bosses who say this often mean your job is to make him *feel* good. They're communicating their need for yes-men, instead of soliciting intelligent and critical participation by their employees. You need to add value in your functional position, partner with him, and make the company stronger. That may mean challenging him, bringing up issues he hasn't thought of, telling him when things aren't going well, or suggesting alternative strategies to what he has proposed. If you just agree with him all the time and pat him on the back to tell him how great he is, what contributions are you making? None, except making him feel good, and that's not your job.

Ironically, in my experience, a guy who says that your job is to make him look good rarely adopts that attitude himself when he's working with his boss—quite the contrary, he usually seems to think his job is to make his boss look *terrible*. So, it's really a self-centered preoccupation, rather than a true belief about subordinate behavior—in other words, it's all about him.

There will be times when your boss doesn't agree with you about an issue and won't take your advice. Don't get mad at him. He might be doing the best he can, and he may know more than you. Don't be a sore loser. Let go, and let him drive. That's why he gets paid the big bucks. I'm often surprised by how critical employees are of their bosses as though he worked for them, instead of the other way around. He's the boss; that's why he's called "The Boss."

I've heard some employees complain when their manager takes credit for their work. You bet! That's how it works. You work for him, and he takes the credit (and responsibility) for your work and the whole team's output. If he's a good manager, he'll never blame you for poor work; that's his responsibility. But, on the flip side, he gets to take credit for your output. If he's a very inclusive manager, he may mention your contribution to his peers and superiors, but he doesn't have to.

Talk to Him

Don't underestimate the importance of your manager, either during the time you work for him or later in your career. These relationships can endure your entire career, even after you've left the company or retired. A good boss is a truly wonderful phenomenon in your work life. While you're reporting to him, he may be working hard behind the scenes to set up your next move or recommending you for an important strategic position. Make sure he knows what your interests are and that you talk with him at least once a year about your next move and what skills you need for a new position.

Again, you may need to initiate these discussions, so he knows you can talk about your ambitions and qualifications in a non-emotional, forthright way. Male managers and subordinates have these conversations more spontaneously because they expect, usually correctly, they can have a frank conversation without any emotional residue. Your boss may not feel he can make that assumption with you, and you don't want to miss out on this important conversation because he's not sure how to bring it up with you. Guys assume other guys are ambitious. They're not as sure about women.

Treat His Spouse with Kid Gloves

Let's talk about your boss's spouse because this can be touchy. Use your head. She has undoubtedly heard quite a bit about you. Heck, your boss has probably told her more about what you've done—good and bad—than he has told you. Most wives of executives are shrewd, observant, and well-informed. Even if she doesn't work outside the home, don't talk down to her. And recognize she'll be very curious about your relationship with her husband because you probably spend more time with him than she does. Also, consider that she may find you threatening, if you're a well-educated professional woman, and she's not. So, watch your step, and don't say foolish, flip things. Take her seriously, and she'll do the same for you. Your boss will probably ask *her* what her impression was; be sure she'll give you a good report. Treat her as you would any other professional colleague.

Be Kind

Male managers are often a little afraid of their female subordinates because they're worried about what *could* happen—she could get mad at him and not tell him, she could register a complaint against him, she could badmouth him behind his back. There's much less assumed trust with a female employee than with a male staff member. It behooves you to be honest and open with your boss so he knows where you stand on things. Help him out. Try to make his relationship with you easy. Try to overlook his shortcomings, not dwell on them. And try to get the most out of each relationship. You may not realize until years later the importance of what he taught you and how lucky you were to work for him.

The Good Guys

We talked in the beginning of the book about the gentlemen who have helped women along their path to equality, those who supported the women's suffrage movement, and those who recognized it was right and good that women be liberated from gender discrimination. Sometimes we forget that, long before the Nineteenth Amendment passed, women were already voting in an extraordinary number of Western states because *men* had given them the right via voter referendum. There are many such remarkable men in the world, and I hope you meet lots of them.

How Many Ways

You may have a manager who takes a special interest in you and makes sure that you're given an important opportunity or included in a select star-employee classification. Someone may volunteer to help you network when you're job-hunting. A senior executive may be keeping an eye on you during your career because he has seen something he likes. Men who sit on your board of directors may be pushing for more gender equality at the senior executive level. Directly or indirectly, all these gentlemen are helping you, and they deserve your appreciation.

Having benefited throughout my career from assistance from men, I feel an obligation to point out that most of the men you work with will help you—though some more than others. Some male executives wisely recognize they shouldn't limit their company's talent pool to one gender and work hard to ensure that rising women are as trained, challenged, and taken care of as the men are. Some corporate executives have young daughters, and they treat you as they hope their daughters will be treated someday. Sometimes a man has hired you, and he feels responsible for your success. Some men help you just because they're kind-hearted and care about young, motivated people. These are all great reasons for you to accept their help. Just don't forget to say thank you and acknowledge that you wouldn't be as far along in your career without their assistance.

Could You Do Me a Favor?

There's no secret about getting help from one of these Good Guys. It's easy—just ask. It's an advantage to have a referral from someone, but it's not necessary. Just call him up or send an email. Be completely honest and upfront about your request. Don't pretend he's going to get something out of it. And don't use your feminine wiles to talk him into something. You don't want any misunderstanding about what you're looking for.

Be clear about what you want, though in some cases, you might just be looking for a networking opportunity and advice. If that's the case, suggest that you get together for coffee or a quick meeting, "just to talk." If you want something more specific, ask upfront, rather than springing it on him later. If you want an introduction to someone, or information, or for him to look at your resumé, go ahead and ask right away. He might be able to help you out, on the spot, which saves him time.

He Might Say No

Before you pop the question, though, prepare yourself because most of time, he'll turn you down. That's just how it goes—these people are busy, and they themselves recognize they can't help everyone. Don't take it personally. It doesn't mean he isn't a Good Guy. Don't be offended if he doesn't even respond. No response does means no, but it's easier than having to call you back and think up an excuse that doesn't sound too rude. He doesn't have an obligation to you since you're asking *him* for a favor. But don't get discouraged. Somewhere along the way, someone will go out of their way to help you, and when they do, you'll be pleased and honored.

Gee, Thanks

When I was thinking of leaving my first corporation, I enlisted the help of five Good Guys, all busy senior people, mostly former colleagues, although a few were referrals from others. I called them "The Committee." Over the next few months, as I reviewed various job opportunities, I ran them past The Committee and got feedback from everyone. Their advice differed from person to person (as you'd hope—otherwise you don't really need a committee), but it was invaluable. After I'd chosen my next position, I sent each of them a pen as a token of my appreciation. I kept in touch with many of them over the years, and one man in particular was always helpful and friendly and mentioned several times that it was his favorite pen. He and I never met in person. You may be amazed by how kind people are who don't even know you.

Women are often good at asking for help, while men may think it's a sign of weakness. Hence all the jokes about why men won't ask for directions. Much has been made of women's reticence to negotiate, but sometimes they're more willing to get help. It's flattering to be asked for help or advice. It implies you're knowledgeable. If asking for help comes easily to you, you're one of the lucky ones.

Extra Good Guys

I'd also add to the list of Good Guys that unusual gentleman who realizes it helps his corporation if he learns how to work with women and makes an effort to understand the differences between men's and women's styles. There are even Good Guys who attempt to alter *their* behavior in order to communicate better with women. When I was in graduate school, I organized a workshop called *Understanding Gender Differences in the Workplace* and was quite surprised when a number of young men showed up. Now that's open-minded for you! I remember an unrelated incident, when one poor soul asked me during a Q&A session, how he could convey to women that he was on their side. He said that because he was an older white guy, they always assumed he was a chauvinist. I asked him if he was looking for something like a password or a secret handshake.

"Yeah!" he said enthusiastically. I told him to keep on doing the right thing, and that actions speak louder than words.

"They'll catch on," I told him. I hope I was right. A guy like that deserves to be well-treated.

International Guys

When you work with non-American guys, you step into a quagmire of cultural and ethical differences on top of the gender issues we've been discussing. And if you figure out how to work with guys from one country—France for example—those insights won't help you if you need to work with someone from a different country—China or Norway. Those guys are completely different! Feel like giving up yet?

I've suggested that you go to work for an American company upon graduation, so you don't have to face all these hurdles right away. As your career develops, however, even if you continue to work for American companies, you'll probably find yourself working with men from other cultures. If you take an overseas assignment, you'll be working with international guys in their home country, and that's harder because you're an alien from several angles. Here are some ways to make it easier.

¿Habla Castellano?

Learn a bit of his language if you can. Speaking his language is a big benefit and will give you some familiarity with the culture. Try to learn enough in order to listen to native speakers talking to each other and get a sense for the emotional pitch of the conversation. Are they discouraged, upset, or arguing? Or is the tone typical for a normal business conversation? These perceptions can provide insight in negotiating or interpreting their reactions. For instance, a friend once told me if Japanese men let out a puff of air—no problem, but if they take a sharp breath—*bad*.

D'oú Venez-vous?

Be interested in his culture. Ask questions about his country. Pay attention to relevant news events. Don't avoid talking about his home as though it's unmentionable. If he's in the U.S., he feels even more out of place than you do. Read up a bit to get a feel for obvious cultural differences and business practices. It might give you a clue as to how comfortable he is working with a woman. If working women are rare in his home country, he may be quite unclear how to behave around you. If he comes from a progressive country with lots of working women, he'll be more at ease and you can assume more about how you can behave around him.

Where Did You Get that Tie?

Be cautious about asking personal questions. People from other cultures don't share their personal life as though it's an open book, the way Americans do. Sometimes American women come on a bit too strong because they're interested and want to be friendly. Do more listening and observing in the beginning until you see how open he is.

Are You Married?

On the other hand, don't be surprised if *they* ask questions you consider inappropriate. In other countries, it's common to ask job applicants their age and whether they have children or intend to have children. In Europe, jobs are posted with an age range. If you're too old—sorry—you can't apply. As a result, guys from other countries may not realize these questions are "loaded" in America. You might want to think about how you would handle these types of questions. I just answered them honestly and didn't react to them. I'm not convinced that making these questions "illegal" in the U.S. has helped us much anyway, since hiring managers simply get the answers by asking somebody who knows the applicant personally.

You're Standing on My Foot

International guys have different cultural norms about personal space and personal hygiene. If you feel as though a guy is crowding you physically, stay open-minded. He may be accustomed to standing very close to someone he's talking to. Unfortunately, he may also not change his clothes or shower as frequently as an American guy, in which case it can be a bit of a double-whammy. Before you denigrate his slovenly personal habits, consider that he's saving water and may be greener than you.

Shall We Go Pubbing?

Be careful about drinking. In my experience, business people from certain countries participate in heavy drinking more frequently than Americans. Although they may be more tolerant of drunken behavior—at least by men—than we are, don't let your guard down. If you participate in after-hours socializing, keep close track of how many drinks you've had and stop before you get drunk. Some guys think it's fun to try to get a woman drunk. Don't get lured into drinking games or drinking cocktails with an unknown alcohol content just because you want to get along with everyone. You can't go with the flow on this one, sister.

The Messed-Up Ones

What if you encounter someone you just plain don't like? This is hard because we have an obligation to work with our colleagues, and sometimes they're downright repellent. Guys who are insecure, suspicious, maimed, or just losers, are no fun to be around. It's easy to feel that you shouldn't have to put up with their flaws, but unfortunately, it's a necessary evil. Perhaps these suggestions will make your days with them a little easier.

Find the Positive

When I was in graduate school, I met a woman at a conference who seemed incredibly misplaced in her company. She was a slightly reformed hippy, working for Exxon in Texas—in the belly of the beast. She described her problems working with a particularly cantankerous co-worker who was loud, rude, and unpleasant. She knew she had to find a way to work with the guy, but everything about him rubbed her the wrong way. She finally set herself the challenge of finding *one* thing about him that she liked. That one positive nugget? He was a good father. After that, when he acted badly and irritated her, she reminded herself to focus on that positive fact so they could have a reasonable working relationship. It's a bit of a mind game, but it works.

He's Still Human

People who behave terribly at work are often—surprisingly—fine, sensitive people off-work, and you'd likely have no trouble getting along with them if they were part of your personal life. People can get confused at work and behave in unnatural and unpleasant ways because of insecurity or misplaced aggression. If you break down those artificial barriers and get to know the person more genuinely, you can compartmentalize their poor behavior and focus on the real character they accidentally let leak through.

Practice Empathy

We're all working in the belly of the beast when we're in a minority. There will be some beastly elements that we have to identify and practice coping with. You can't let them fester and harp about how terrible they are—that won't help you. To work cooperatively, you need a less judgmental attitude.

I'll appeal to your more generous side here. It won't hurt you to soften your heart a bit and be more forgiving in your observations.

People are sometimes remarkably unhappy, which leads to all kinds of bad behavior at work. If people are new in their jobs, never got an advanced degree, aren't as tall as they wanted, or are still trying to impress their father—all these unresolved insecurities can manifest themselves in a guy who is difficult to work with. Some people have terrible problems: toxic marriages, delinquent or damaged children, tragedies in the past, twisted childhoods, wicked parents... Some people harbor awful secrets and fight ferocious demons. Try taking a kinder view of why they are the way they are. It doesn't make you a weaker person or less likely to succeed if you give your colleagues the benefit of the doubt and overlook their shortcomings. Remember, you're the one who takes the high road, who is bigger than they are, stronger and tougher. Think of yourself as a big powerful lioness with a huge heart, focused on business, and undeterred by petty blows.

A word of caution here: While I see empathy as a positive trait, guys don't like people to feel sorry for them. They think it puts them in an inferior position. One boss made this clear. We'd gotten into a messy personnel situation that wasn't anyone's fault—just a case of bad chemistry between two people.

"I feel so sorry for everyone," I said sadly to the CEO.

"Eww," he responded with disgust. He looked as though he'd just stepped in something.

Be careful how you express empathy, but don't stop feeling it.

Don't Write Him Off

One of my faults is that it's hard for me to suffer fools. When someone is acting stupid, I have a tendency to get on my high horse and point it out. My kids call me "Hermione" for a reason. Fortunately, an observant boss pointed this out early in my career so I was constantly on guard and taught myself to keep the safety on and hold my tongue. That worked pretty well until I ran up against a co-worker who *really* bugged me. He was arrogant, autocratic, and couldn't be bothered to learn the business. He dictated senseless new procedures from afar and then wouldn't return phone calls. I tried to establish a relationship with him for about a year. Then I gave up and *wrote him off.* Oops. Sure enough, it showed up on every performance appraisal I got after that. "Weak relationship with Colin. Needs to build bridges. Jennifer must improve the communication channels with division controller..."

"But he's unreasonable," I complained to my boss. "And it's a one-way street."

"I know, I know," my boss explained, "but you *have* to find a way to make it work."

In retrospect, I can clearly see my error was that I gave up. Once I'd gotten it into my head that it was impossible, I stopped trying, and that's really what I was being reprimanded for. And rightly so.

Get Close

Okay, so the *next* time I encountered someone like that, I could see right away he was going to get under my skin, and I plotted accordingly. Although he was a different generation and nationality, he displayed the same imperiousness, surliness, and pleasure in running roughshod over the employees that really *push my buttons.* So, I got close. Keep your enemies close? Heck, I practically moved into his office. I wore a path in the carpet between my office and his—after every dysfunctional meeting, hostile phone mail message, or insulting email, first thing in the morning, last thing every night, I connected with him in person. And I got to know him. And he got to know me.

"He likes you," my boss said, puzzled. "That's very unusual."

Heh heh. My plan worked perfectly. By spending more time with him, I saw how to help and impress him. I became more sympathetic as I saw how frustrated he was by everything that was thrown at him and how he suffered from desperation and fear. By being at his elbow every minute, I could influence his behavior on the spot instead of reacting to it afterward. I also discovered that his staff wasn't offering any alternatives to his hair-brained ideas because they were afraid of him, and he didn't know how to ask for help. To my surprise, he was open to suggestions.

"Okay, that sounds rational," he would say slowly. "We'll try it your way. But if it doesn't work, I'm blaming you!"

That was fine. I knew my ideas would work. We managed to establish a wavering partnership that got stronger the longer we worked together. Don't be afraid to co-opt these Messed-Up guys. Whether it's your side or his side, you just want to get on the *same* side.

Bad Guys

It's important to talk openly about the troubles you may encounter working with men, but these next sections won't be very fun to read. I don't want to discourage you, but I prefer you to be forewarned and to have thought through how you might handle these nasty guys. I learned about some of them the hard way, and I want you to be better prepared than I was. Sorry to generalize–every guy you encounter will be unique in his own twisted way, but learning the identifying marks will help you plan your defense strategies.

Ogres

These guys aren't that bad, but they disguise themselves as Bad Guys. I've met a number of these guys, and I presume you will, too. They're grumpy men, usually with fierce reputations, who seem to go around hopping mad all the time. They bite people's heads off, their colleagues hate dealing with them, their fiery tempers spoil the office environment, and their work problems are all smushed up into one giant dysfunctional ball. Now it turns out you have to work with one of them. Great.

I encountered an ogre when I was put on an international task force with a country manager. He was European, but the tales of his temper tantrums were global. He was short, loud, and always furious, as far as I could tell. I dreaded the first time we had to travel together. And here's what happened. He asked me politely if I would mind if we drove. I was surprised since we normally flew to that location, and I wasn't happy about the length of the trip, or the close quarters, but I was looking for any way to get on his good side, so I reluctantly said yes. After he'd picked me up, he asked politely if he could play some music; I said yes. And he put in Bach's French Suites, which almost moved him into Good Guy category on the spot—I love those pieces. Over the next few hours, I saw a different man emerge. I began to understand how his recent loss of authority, combined with his age and ego, was frustrating and threatening to him in a way he didn't know how to handle. He wasn't that bad of a guy, but he was extremely sensitive and lacked self-control.

Eventually, I developed some velvet gloves and figured out how to work with him. Sometimes I just had to wait until he'd calmed down. I asked him once, "Why are you yelling?" He responded, suddenly dejected, "I'm kind of a tense person." You don't say. Over time, as he saw that I didn't take his outbursts personally and I wasn't going away, he came to trust me and sometimes confide in me. He was hard to work with, but he taught me a lot. He had some positive characteristics—he was smart, observant, and well-read—but he masked them in ogre clothing.

Liars

In my experience, a lot of men tell lies. Unlike most women, men don't seem to have the same scrupulous belief that every little word out of their mouths has to be completely accurate. Guys seem to feel comfortable bragging about what they've done in the past, even when it doesn't jive with the facts. It's as though they can change the past by telling a different story. They may feel that a little exaggeration regarding their exploits is expected and that everyone enhances their successes. It's just storytelling, after all. I call these "fish stories." A common one is the "and then I said to him..." tale where his side of the conversation now shows how brilliant he is. Others are stories in which he takes individual credit for something accomplished by the entire team, stories that overstate his financial success, stories of accolades that sound much bigger than they really were, etc. Have you heard stories like these, especially in job interviews? Depending on your level of tolerance, you might not be thrilled with this kind of self-aggrandizing, but it seems pretty common among men in the business world.

Beyond a tendency to spin past achievements, exaggeration can move up to the level I'd classify as "lies." Men will brag that a product they launched sold $100 million when it didn't. They'll tell you they personally made $10 million when their company was sold when they didn't. They'll claim they held a certain position at a company when they didn't. They'll modify their resumé to make it look as though they worked for a particular company when they didn't. I'm surprised by how much lying there is, and I don't want you to engage in it, but don't be too shocked by it, either. These kinds of lies are so common that I wouldn't even classify the guys who tell them as Bad Guys though you want to keep an eye on them anyway.

What about really black lies—nasty buggers that leap from the mouths of men to mislead and manipulate? These are a *big problem* because when the liar deliberately chooses to distort the facts, he's helping himself to the upper hand in the relationship and sacrificing an equal partnership in which real information is shared openly. With liars, you can't get a fair resolution because you don't have access to complete information. He's manipulating you into a win-lose outcome. That's why lying is disrespectful and evil.

Here are some examples: Suppose your boss tells you that none of your peers received a salary increase, but you find out that several people did get increases, although you weren't one of them. Or the CEO tells you he recommended you for a promotion, but the board rejected it; you find out later that, in fact, the CEO recommended that you *not* be promoted. What if the medical director claims relevant clinical data weren't available at the time of a press release, but it turns out later that they were. Those are big lies and can't be tolerated.

Some bosses lie to you because they don't want to deal with your reaction to the truth—or so they claim. Or they may excuse it by saying they were just protecting you, or because someone else told them they *had* to lie. They may even try to restate what they said so it's not a lie anymore. Regardless of the reason, these are Bad Guys. They're not just lying to impress you; they want to manipulate you, get something from you, or because they're weak. If you catch someone in a lie, pay attention. This very bad sign can't be taken lightly. Don't give them the benefit of the doubt. Sometimes female executives forgive too easily. In my experience, liars do so with no compunction, and they're repeat offenders. Liars lie. Once you have identified a liar, don't believe anything he says.

Cheaters and Thieves

Guys in this category falsify their expense reports, steal computers and phones, take their buddies out to dinner with company money, play fast and loose with gifts for "customers," and make the company pay for upgrades in plane tickets and rental cars when it's against company policy. They're willing to cross ethical lines because they think they're above the rules. Sometimes you uncover a whole culture of Cheaters and Thieves in certain departments where the behavior is excused because "everyone does it." Make no mistake—not everyone is doing it. It's wrong, it's not in the shareholders' best interest, and it shouldn't be tolerated. These are Bad Guys who hurt the company and you.

How can you deal with cheaters and thieves? It depends on your position and the company. Many organizations have a whistleblower process to protect you from retaliation if you tell on someone. If there's no formal process, you may have to choose carefully whom you talk to so you don't suffer a backlash. Consider if the company will take action or not. If not, think about how far-reaching this culture is and ask yourself if you want to stay there. No one would expect you to risk your reputation if no good will come of it—you may just want to move on. You may decide it's limited to a few people, and you don't want to sacrifice yourself for a few clowns. But be conscious that you have identified those individuals as cheaters and thieves. Different circumstances dictate different strategies, but you must recognize these Bad Guys for what they are, and don't ignore what they've done.

If you've discovered that a cheater reports to you, you have no choice—you have to take action. You may decide to give the cheater a second chance, but make it clear that this behavior is unacceptable and that you'll fire him if he does it again.

By the way, in my experience, men who talk about how ethical they are often aren't. In fact, quite the opposite, the more a guy talked about how ethical he was, the less ethical he was! You should ignore that kind of chest-beating.

Bullies

If you work with a lot of men, you're likely to encounter a bully. These insecure men try to get their way by force and intimidation. They use their body and their voice in a threatening manner to cow other employees and get them to back down. They're quick to anger and have found that yelling and threatening are effective tools in the workplace. In my experience, they aren't very bright and suffer from a lack of verbal skills. When they're outgunned intellectually or verbally, they resort to bullying to gain a superior position. They tend to be emotional and unhappy.

Sadly, you can feel sorry for a bully, but you can't put up with him. Yelling and threatening behaviors create a bad work environment. People who work for a bully won't confront him; they disengage, and the company suffers from their lack of involvement. Some people prefer to leave than put up with a bully. In many ways, bullies cost the company money.

Some men only bully "down" the organization; they focus on people who are lower on the totem pole. But don't be surprised if someone tries to bully you even if you're at a higher level than he is. Some men prefer to bully a woman because she's an easy target, and they think she won't fight back. If this happens to you, what are your options?

First, identify the behavior as true bullying. Bullying isn't just yelling—there's lots of yelling at work that isn't bullying. Bullying is when you can never have a civilized disagreement with him, and he always resorts to violence and threatening behavior to get his way. When someone consistently yells at you as a way to shut you up, that's bullying. He's trying to keep you from doing your job.

Once you've made a positive I.D., choose your strategy. You could start by telling him he's a bully and see if he can stop it once he's been outed. You might also try yelling back—not out of control, but really loud—to see what happens. To my enormous surprise, that has actually worked for me. For some reason, my bullies just folded once I yelled at them. I was truly flabbergasted. If that doesn't work, you may have to get human resources or your management involved. You can't just put up with it. It hinders your ability to do your job, so it has to be stopped.

Woman-Haters

Have you ever encountered someone who was rude to you from the moment he or she met you for no apparent reason? Have you heard someone make a surprisingly nasty comment about your looks, authority, or activities that seemed honestly uncalled for? Or there's a tone a person uses with you that implies you're not entirely on the up-and-up? Aha! You may be in the presence of a woman-hater. They come in both male and female varieties and are more common than you think. Many people have woman-hating tendencies that they let go of once they get to know you. Other people will quickly revert to their misogyny when you're under attack and they lose faith in you.

For our purposes, I'll focus on the male variety. First (you knew I was going to say this), have a little sympathy. The guy may have an awful mom or a hateful wife. People generalize from what they know specifically, and he probably didn't have a good experience with women in his early life. He may know intellectually that there are fine women out there, but he'll start out assuming the worst. That's pretty logical, and you might, too, if you were in his shoes. But you should do everything in your power to prove him wrong. Always take the high road, and don't debase yourself around him. If he insinuates that you have ulterior motives, call him on it. Say, "That's not true." Be honest and truthful and speak your mind. Who knows, maybe he'll eventually begrudgingly acknowledge you're a real person and not a stereotype.

I worked with a guy who I thought must be a woman-hater because he never had a good word to say about any woman and his criticisms had a sexual, derogatory overtone. I was wrong about him. After we had worked together for a while, I realized he was perplexed by women, and he tested them to see if they were for real or not. Once I passed his hazing, he was a powerful advocate and friend to this day. There are lots of woman-haters out there, but don't be too quick to label a colleague as one.

If someone is too biased to be convinced you're not evil, try to overlook the snide comments. Some people don't realize how prejudiced they sound when they trash-talk about the First Lady or

Nancy Pelosi or whatever powerful woman they feel threatened by. It's a mindless habit with them as it used to be when people made racist comments (or still do). It's not personal, so you don't need to respond to it as though it were.

Harassers

The closest I came to getting raped at work was when I had a job detasseling corn in Indiana as a teenager. Don't laugh—in the olden days, farmers employed young people to walk through muddy corn fields, pulling out the yellow flowers that grow at the top of a corn plant and throwing them on the ground. It was sticky, sweaty, dirty work, and tempers and libidos ran hot. Corporate America can pose some harassment risks, but it shouldn't be *that* bad.

Sexual harassment on the job is defined as any unwelcome sexually oriented behavior, demand, comment, or physical contact initiated by an individual at the workplace that is a term or condition of employment, a basis for employment decisions, or that interferes with the employee's work or creates a hostile or offensive working environment.

This is a legal definition, including lots of fine points that can be argued about and analyzed and clarified in court. For you, girlfriend, I would say this: If you feel as though you're being harassed at work, don't put up with it, don't hope it will just go away, and take action to make it stop. If you're having this kind of trouble, my heart goes out to you. It can ruin your work life. But women too often simply put up with it, and guess what—it goes on and on.

Not every physical contact is harassment, although some men pretend that's what fuddy-duddy lawyers have tried to impose on them. Those guys are impostors—they know what's okay and what's not. They just don't want any rules placed on their behavior. On the contrary, nice guys will sometimes touch you, and if they're nice, you won't mind. If someone puts his arm around you to show you he's proud of you, hugs you when you're leaving for a long trip, pats you on the back when you've done a good job, high-fives you after a good presentation, those gestures aren't sexual and are meant to communicate, not harass. My male colleagues who weren't especially articulate would sometimes communicate in those ways—it was hard for them to put their emotions into words, so they expressed themselves more physically. I was never uncomfortable with their touching me. For me, it was always crystal clear whether I was dealing with a Good Guy, a rat, or someone who had gotten confused (usually by drinking). Spend some time thinking about what is and is not acceptable to you. Then you can react fast when some guy touches you.

Here's my rule of thumb: If there's physical contact that makes you uncomfortable, it's harassment, and you should tell him to cut it out. *And right now.* If someone's touching you in an inappropriate way at work, tell him to stop it, clearly and loudly, and in someone else's presence. Jerk away from him; don't let his hands stay on you. Knock his hand off if you have to. This has always worked for me, but if that doesn't stop it, don't give up. Keep telling him to stop it, and raise the pressure by going to someone else in the company. You're the best judge of whom to appeal to first, but your options include: human resources, your manager, his manager, or anyone else who will take you seriously and recognize that you need protection.

I heard an amazing story from a young woman who was being harassed by her boss. She said he would "put his hands all over me when we slow-danced." Huh? Why on earth are you *dancing* with him, honey? Say NO. Stand up for yourself! Don't just suffer.

If there's no physical contact, and the harassment is all verbal, recognize that this will be harder for you to explain and for others to understand. You still shouldn't put up with it, but be aware it will be harder to prove and to prohibit. These situations can be complicated, so it's hard to give good advice here, but I would say if you feel constantly uncomfortable and can identify certain behaviors that you wish would stop, that your harasser engages in *regularly*, you should tell the offender specifically what he must stop doing. He may just stop, or he may get antagonistic and more focused in his harassment. Although that will be harder in the short term, it's better to have more specific discussion points to object to and ask for help in stopping.

My experience with men crossing over into inappropriate territory was usually one-off situations with guys who were vaguely hostile at work but then got a few drinks in them. Read the "After Hours" section for general advice about how to protect yourself. I wasn't above using other men in the group to shield me from the harasser, even putting them physically between me and him. Good Guys are often pretty aware of what's going on under the surface and will move in to shut off the harasser once they're sure you have no interest.

These situations are delicate and subtle, but the biggest mistake you can make when you suspect you're being harassed is not doing anything about it. Be cognizant that the person who will be most effective in getting it to stop is *you*. You can't just make a complaint about someone behind his back and expect the harassment to magically end. You have to be involved, and you have to provide very specific information. Especially, don't let it get started, put up with it, and *then* try to stop it. You need to be aggressive right away. It's much harder to stop once it's gotten a foothold. I do hope you never find yourself caught up in this ugliness.

Super Bad Guys

There are Super Bad Guys out there who have lost their moral compass, break the law, lie and charm easily, steal and cheat, and take advantage of others. They want to get ahead at all costs. They're in a separate class from Bad Guys because their unethical behavior crosses over into many parts of their lives, and in some cases, their behavior is criminal. Under desperate circumstances, some people will push themselves to commit acts they would normally not commit. Other people have a long history of unethical behavior that permeates their entire life. Regardless of the reason for their problems, you can't hang out with Super Bad Guys. They are extremely dangerous, and they could take you down with them. They can ruin your career and certainly hurt your self-esteem. Some should even go to jail.

They're Out There

Sadly, these guys exist in corporate America. They're extraordinarily talented and ruthless, and you may not realize they are, oh, so much better than you at watching and observing and manipulating. They don't care about you; they only see you as a potential conquest, either financially or sexually, or as someone they can use. This type of guy doesn't have a grasp on reality. He doesn't acknowledge who he is; he doesn't question his own behavior. He acts out of habits that have been reinforced by a lifetime of deceit and narcissism. He lives in a different world, one created by delusions. Alcoholism, womanizing, gambling, and a street-fighting approach to business often seem to be part of the package.

What's a girl to do? First, be smart. Super Bad Guys usually have a reputation and a history. Because these habits are not new, if you ask around, you'll discover the guy is associated with accusations of cheating, harassing, and even fraud. Back away from him—don't try to fix him. His problems are far too severe for your kind and well-meaning heart. You can't stop him either; you're not the police. You can warn people about him, but I wouldn't try to put an end to his deceitful career. You have to assume he will eventually get his comeuppance, and in the meantime, you have better things to do. Stay away from Super Bad Guys.

Identifying Marks

If you suspect you're dealing with a Super Bad Guy, watch for these signs. Does he brag about tricking people, especially financially? Does he seem to have an unusually high level of debt or seem desperate to make it big? Is he overly preoccupied with wealth and rich people? Does he propose complicated financial arrangements and appear unimpressed when he's told they're illegal? Does he snicker about people who lie to the government? Does he openly admit he cheats on his taxes? Does he have a history of having been investigated? Does he heavy-handedly try to force self-serving conclusions even when the facts don't support them? Does he have a history of working for disreputable companies or with disreputable people? Is he constantly jockeying for a more favorable position in business transactions? Does he have slime ball friends?

Be cautious when you are dealing with businessmen from other cultures. American ideas of fair business practices are not global, and some cultures are more tolerant of bribery, fraud, and corruption. Men from other countries sometimes don't have the same dim view of under-handed business dealings that I do. These guys don't get why America has laws forbidding foreign corrupt practices and aren't particularly inclined to obey them. Watch out for guys who seem cavalier about American securities laws or about rules in general. They may be willing to take more risks than you would, but they're still gambling with your career.

If you run across one of these guys, I hope it's during the job interview process and *before* you've gone to work with him. Some Super Bad Guys have risen to pretty high levels in an organization, so don't assume that just because he's at a senior level, he must be okay. Listen hard for these red flags when you're contemplating changing jobs, and don't ignore them if you hear them. Ask around about him outside of the company. Make contact with people who used to work with him but who have moved on. Try to talk to the person who held the job before you. Listen for code words when people describe him—"a real dynamo," "He could sell snow to the Eskimos," or "I actually felt sorry for the guys on the other side." These are not necessarily positive reports, and you may be being warned.

Extraordinary Skills—Used for Evil

People who are very good at negotiating and reading people can also be those who don't have a clear understanding of right and wrong. It's not surprising, but it is scary, because it means your enemy is formidable and ruthless. This guy, when he's told no, will try to move the goalposts so maybe "no" doesn't really mean "no."

Do you know somebody who just won't take no for an answer? How about someone who restates something he's been told in order to gain an edge or put a different spin on the message? Do you know a strong negotiator who somehow seems to be able to get the other party to put something back on the table when you thought it was completely off? Now, you can see how these extraordinary negotiating skills could be used against you.

Super Bad Guys don't change their spots; that's why a sexual predator often has a terrible reputation as a womanizer and exploiter. Don't assume you'll get through to the good side of him; don't fool yourself into thinking you understand him in ways other women don't. If he has taken advantage of other women (including his wife), he'll take advantage of you. Don't be fooled by a charming and warm exterior—he didn't become a master manipulator by being transparently evil! If you're paying attention and not trying to fool yourself, it's not that hard to unmask him. You'll see it's easy to catch him in a lie or that he has left a whole series of women behind who are ashamed of their association with him and acknowledge they were vulnerable and exploited.

I went to work for a company that employed a known predator, and I asked about him during the interview process.

"Oh no, he's changed," one of his colleagues told me. "He's had health issues, so he's changed his ways."

Ha. I'd only been there a few weeks when I discovered that not only had he not changed his ways, but he was harassing one of *my* employees. I was furious and confronted the head of human resources. To her credit, she and the board took action immediately to get rid of him, but it didn't take him long to land at a new company, despite his reputation and dismissal.

Super Bad Guys are often tolerated in corporate America, and boards and management teams look the other way when they're otherwise pleased with an executive's performance. You wouldn't think this would be true in this age of litigation, but it's surprisingly persistent. So, don't be too trusting, look for identifying marks, and know your enemy.

CHAPTER EIGHT

You're a Big Girl Now

YOU MUST WORK WELL with men to be successful in most corporations, but producing exceptional work is how you differentiate yourself and ultimately how you drive up your compensation and improve your job satisfaction. This chapter addresses ways in which you can stand out from the typical mediocrity that exists in middle management, by becoming an outstanding manager and avoiding common mistakes. We also take a look at special problems that executive women often face in the middle stages of their career.

Managing—Between a Rock and a Hard Place

When I became a manager, I thought middle management positions must be the most difficult because you have tremendous responsibility, but are trapped between the hourly workers and the executives. You can't delegate upward because your tasks are so tactical that most executives would be incapable of performing them. Can you imagine asking some vice president to run payroll? And you can't delegate much downward because the hourly employees' jobs are very strictly defined and routine, and they can't handle ad-hoc problems that require creativity to solve. So, there you are, until 9 o'clock at night, coping with everything that's really hard: broken equipment, computer errors, angry customers, a fistfight in the parking lot... Everything seems to fall on your plate. Then I moved into general management and found out it was even worse!

On the other hand, I found personnel management to be the most rewarding part of my job. It's not easy because people are infinitely complicated (and fascinating), but the joy of developing people, the power of a productive team, and the satisfaction with a group's accomplishments can create memories that last a lifetime. A team really is bigger than its parts, and figuring out how to form a group of individuals into a team and motivate them is quite inspiring. It also made me incredibly happy to watch an employee gain skills and confidence and to think, "I was part of that." I hope you take on these tough jobs with high expectations and that your efforts are mightily rewarded.

Reporting Lines Must Be Clear

First, you must know who reports to you and to whom you report. Each employee should have one solid reporting line to one other company employee. No one should report to consultants or to people outside the organizational chart. Dotted reporting lines, through which an employee has responsibilities to a different manager from his or her supervisor, should be avoided, especially more than one. They cause confusion and sometimes only exist to placate someone's ego. The hierarchy and relationships must be clear. Don't tolerate any wooliness about a reporting line just because you're trying to be accommodating.

The human resources department should be on your side here, but occasionally you'll run into a personnel manager who just wants "everyone to get along," and won't force the hard decisions that would straighten out a garbled reporting line. At the very least, make sure you understand what performance reviews you'll be writing, what influence you'll have over someone's salary, and whether you're responsible for day-to-day assignments. If someone reports to you, you should have all three responsibilities. Don't get in a position where you're responsible for someone's assignments but not their performance evaluation—that's a recipe for disaster.

Defy the "Bitch" Stereotype

People prefer to report to men by a wide margin, so tread gently when you become someone's boss. They probably aren't thrilled at the news, and it will be up to you to defy the stereotype of the bad female boss.

Men especially don't like reporting to women. They may not like being in a subordinate position to a woman, or they may have some anxieties about how they're supposed to behave. You might be their first female boss, and they may be concerned about what that says about them. They'll have heard terrible stories about reporting to women; consequently, they might be pretty nervous. If they're accustomed to being the strong male around women—the problem solver, the provider, the one that women turn to—they'll be confused about how to apply that in a work environment. The usual ways in which they interact with women, socially or with family members, won't work now. How do they ask their female boss for help when women usually ask *them* for help? And do they really have to ask her permission to do something? That's insulting. Imagine how disturbing it is for them to receive a "performance evaluation" from a woman.

Before you panic and run off, let me say I've had really excellent male employees, and they've shown me respectful and effective ways to be their supervisor. Be extremely careful not to bruise your male employee's ego and make him feel inferior. Since male employees are much more sensitive to implied put-downs and imperious commands than female employees, try to avoid any innuendos. Men often understand how to be a member of a sports team, and the language of sports can be useful to explain proper corporate behavior and provide feedback on their performance. Rather than emphasizing their inferior position to me in the hierarchy, I talk about the different positions on the team and my role as coach.

Give Him Some Space

Male employees often deal with their emotions through anger, raised voices, and forceful language. When emotions run high, it's best to give these employees lots of room because they may be trying to tell you something, and often it's an excellent point. If you don't react negatively, but take an unemotional and listening stance, he should eventually calm down and tell you what's wrong. Then you can do something about it. Remember, just because he's yelling doesn't mean it's directed at you. Of course, you have the power to shut him down, but why would you? He needs help, not to be sent back to his cubicle like a bad little boy. And if he needs to yell, it should be in your office where it's safe, not anywhere else in the workplace.

I find humor can help defuse the situation and let him deal with his frustration. With practice, you'll find it pretty easy to move to his side, ask what's going on, how you can help, and eventually make a crack about how his outburst almost made the pictures fall off the wall or how you have to bring ear plugs to work now. He'll appreciate your calm approach and that *his* emotions won't be held against him. If yelling becomes chronic, you'll have to deal with it as a performance issue, but you can do that when he's calm and receptive to feedback, not when he's out of his mind.

Male employees will test you more than female ones, for a variety of reasons: just for fun, because they're bored, to see how tough you are, or to find out if they can trip you up. They may be more outspoken and critical of the organization than the women. A guy is more likely to tell you some corporate policy is asinine, or complain about a new rule, or feel the need to tell you how worthless the regulatory department is. I find that a rational, non-adversarial stance is effective in getting him back on task, reminding him that we're all on the same team and why we're here, without making him feel reprimanded. When guys can't provoke a reaction from you, sometimes they just lose interest.

Your Employees Are Your Business

You're responsible for your employees—their development, success, and happiness. When you become someone's manager, first admit how ignorant you are—you don't know how to do all your employees' jobs, what they're going through, or what they need. Meet with them and tell them they know more than you do. They'll appreciate your willingness to admit what they already knew. Then tell them what the trade is: They teach you about their jobs, and you'll get them what they need.

When you have direct reports, you're responsible for their success, and your job is to support them. You must care for them, help them develop, make sure they're fairly compensated, give them interesting, rewarding projects and the necessary resources and training to succeed. If they have shortcomings, you must develop and improve their performance. I tell my employees my goal is to make sure they have more skills and knowledge in their tool belts when they leave me than they had when they came to me. I remind them to include their accomplishments on their resumé and watch it grow. That's my job.

Part of your job is to coach—to teach your employees how to advocate for themselves. That's not at odds with the company's interest because employees mustn't feel taken advantage of. You may have to coach your female employees differently from the males. Women are socialized not to ask for higher pay or a promotion when it might appear self-interested, and they're acutely aware of the ugliness of being "me-oriented." By teaching your female employees to think about what they *should* be paid, what opportunities they *should* have, and to take responsibility for their own careers, you're ensuring that they feel that their compensation and chances are equitable. In turn, they'll stay with you longer, and the lowered turnover will benefit your company.

As the boss, you are the most important person in your employee's work life. You alone have the power to make it terrible or tolerable. The most common reason people give for leaving an organization is that they didn't like their boss. Take this part of your job seriously. Pay close attention to your employees; check in with them frequently, at least daily. Make sure they know your door is always open to them. Meet with them formally each week, and always do performance appraisals on time—how rude and telling it is when the supervisor is "too busy" to write someone's performance appraisal. Wow, what a message that sends.

Here's a trick to make writing performance appraisals easier. I like to have my employees submit a monthly report to me, limited to one page, that includes bullet points of their accomplishments that month, and what their goals are for the next month. This is a low-key way to provide feedback—positive and negative—about the accomplishments themselves as well as *how* they were achieved. You can make notes in the margin for yourself while you're reviewing the report together during one of your weekly meetings that month. Revisiting the goals every month helps employees stay on track with their annual goals as well as highlight when one has become meaningless or when a more pressing goal should be substituted. The previous month's goals should move up to the accomplishments section on the next month's report. If this isn't occurring, you can find out why and see if procrastination, resources, or a lack of understanding is the problem. Complex goals should be broken down into smaller monthly tasks so the employee isn't overwhelmed by an onerous hurdle staring them in the face.

At the end of the year, you have a great record of the good and the bad, which makes writing the performance appraisal easier and more accurate. That way, you're not overly influenced by something that just happened in the last month and instead can take the whole year into consideration. You can also look for patterns of behavior that showed up over the course of the year and provide useful insights to your employees about their performance. In addition, these monthly reports help the employees, if they're required to write a self-evaluation. Rather than sitting down at the end of the year and trying to remember everything they did, they can easily review their monthly reports and draw from them.

Employees go through ups and downs, just as you do. If you want a long-term employee (and you do), you may have to weather some times when his or her performance takes a turn for the worse. I found it better to be upfront, particularly with men.

During one weekly meeting, for instance, I asked one of my male employees with whom I had a good relationship: "What's going on with you? It seems like your productivity is way down."

"I'm going through a divorce," he said.

Oh. Glad I asked. And a few months later, he was back to his old self.

The bottom line is that the buck stops with you. Their performance, good or bad, is your fault or to your credit. You can't blame your employees for poor performance. It's your responsibility to fix it or get rid of them. It does no good to whine about performance shortcomings—you have to address them. Most managers complain about their employees but shy away from taking positive action. Don't look the other way, and don't give employees the benefit of the doubt for too long.

My boss was once critical of one of my employees, and I found myself defending her. She wasn't a stellar employee, but she wasn't awful.

"*You* wouldn't behave that way," he scowled at me. By golly, he was right about that. What a wakeup call about my own egotism, as though no one could hope to measure up to me. From that point, I started using a different yardstick to measure employee performance.

Be Honest with Your Employees

That's how you build trust. Employees are stunningly perceptive about whether you're telling the truth or not, and they have extraordinary memories. Be aware that they're listening to your every word because what you say affects their livelihood, the most important aspect of their job. They're always on the lookout for bad news, and they feel betrayed when they discover that you hid some from them. Don't try to deceive them and then wiggle out of it. If you're unmasked as a liar, even once, they'll never trust you again. This is hard for managers, especially senior managers, because they want so badly to reassure employees and not let them worry. Too bad—you're better off treating them as adults. They'll appreciate it, and you'll be surprised at how philosophical even lower-level employees can be about negative company news. They think a lot more about the company, how it's run, and what its prospects are than most senior managers realize.

Employees are acutely aware of management's tendency to share good news and spin or hide bad news. In company meetings, they listen carefully, but are often reticent to ask questions. Encourage tough questions, and answer them honestly. That's how you keep rumors and incorrect information from dominating the communication pathways. In the absence of real information, employees just make stuff up (usually negative), and all kinds of crazy rumors run out through the grapevine. I've even gone as far as to model tough questions after my own presentation to employees, to set an example and lighten the tone. If I called for questions, and no one asked what I thought was probably on people's minds, I would say, "Nobody's going to ask me about the lawsuit? Okay, let me show you how you ask tough questions. Tough Question #1: 'Jennifer, I read in the paper that we were sued. What's the company update on that?'" It gave them an opportunity to chuckle and then lean in *very* closely to hear the answer. Eventually, the employees took over the tough questions, and then we would really sweat! But it made for a more productive Q&A session.

Sometimes you can't answer a tough question. You might be legally prohibited, you don't know the answer, it's too early to know, someone's privacy is at stake, outside negotiations are underway, or the data aren't in yet—there can be lots of reasons. In this case, first, try to understand the motivation for asking the question. Do they genuinely have a legitimate need to know, or are they just curious? That will guide you as to how to address a genuine concern or let you know if it's just a prurient interest in someone else's business. In my experience, in an open forum, employees almost always ask questions because they have a legitimate need to know. In private, they might ask questions just because they're curious, but usually, in a big meeting, they don't want to look like a gossip. It's perfectly all right to say, "I can't talk about that," and explain *why*. If it's a good reason, they'll understand and will wait until you can talk about it. Just be sure that you do get back to them, bring up that old tough question, and answer it. Don't let unanswered questions hang around for a long time. Your employees won't forget them, so you'd better not, either.

Talk to Them

Employees often know what needs to be done, and if you ask nicely, they may tell you. Ask all your staff members the same six questions in private. Devise serious questions: "What's the biggest challenge we face? What do you want me to focus on? What's our scariest risk?" I bet you'll be amazed how thoughtful and insightful their responses are, occasionally more astute than those you would get from your board of directors!

Make sure that you appreciate your employees and that they know it. Tell them frequently how important they are and how their good work contributes to the organization. Celebrate their tenure anniversaries as much, or more, than their birthdays. A long-term employee is incredibly valuable, and every year that goes by is something to be proud of. The success of you, your team, and your company depend on your employees. The better they perform, the better the team gets and looks, and the more you excel as a leader. Be extremely attentive to your employees.

I truly believe that people are a company's most valuable assets. Try moving your company to another state, as one company I worked for did, leaving behind all the key employees because they wouldn't leave California, and you'll discover what they did—within six months, there was no company. I think it's strange that a company's two most valuable assets, people and patents, don't show up on its balance sheet. How illogical is that?

Keep your conversations with your employees professional. Don't treat them like your therapist and unload your personal problems on them or chitchat at length with them as though they're your friend. They're not your therapist or your friend, and they don't want to be either. They do want you to behave the way you're supposed to, but they can't come out and tell you that, because it's an unequal relationship. You're the boss. Act like it.

On the other hand, don't make the mistake that I made when I was a beginning manager. Because I took my job very seriously, I didn't share *any* personal details with my staff. I thought they weren't really interested, but would pretend to be, just to be polite. It wasn't until my first 360° assessment, when I got feedback from my subordinates, that I learned they did want to know more about me. In fact, some of them knew so little about me that they didn't even know I was into physical fitness. That really shocked me. How could they not know that? Didn't they see me riding my bike to work? But, of course, they didn't know—I'd never told them. Instead I started being more open about my personal life and getting comfortable with letting the employees know a little more about me. Employees want to feel that they know their leaders—it builds trust and motivation. So don't make my newbie mistake.

Bad Bosses

Warning: Rant follows. It's been pretty well understood over the past few decades how to be a good manager, so I'm just ASTOUNDED at how many TERRIBLE managers there are and how they're TOLERATED in corporate America. It's very disturbing to me to see managers abuse, ignore, blame, denigrate, and take advantage of their employees.

First, don't yell at your employees. It's just terrible to abuse the people who make you successful. Please don't do this. You may have to be firm to be heard or get their attention, but no out-of-control yelling. You can't—because of your superior position to them, they can't yell back which makes it just unfair. Besides, it's your job to uplift them, not yell at them.

Here's an example: I engaged a company to help us write a grant. The junior member of the team sent me a boilerplate email explaining the process. He accidentally addressed me as "Carol," which wasn't a big deal. In fact, I hadn't even noticed *until* I received an email from the poor fellow's boss (who'd been copied on the Carol email) in which he used the f-word and berated the guy for his mistake. How ironic that *his* mistake was to accidentally copy me on his mean email. I felt like sending him an email that said YOU'RE FIRED, but I was afraid it would be blamed on the junior guy who was actually doing a fine job. Too bad he had to work for a JERK.

Don't Hide Their Weaknesses

Here's something else that bad bosses do, and it's not because they're mean—it's because they're weak. They won't tell their employee what he or she is doing wrong. This is such a disservice to someone who *needs* your feedback. I know it's difficult, especially for kind-hearted women, but you have to grit your teeth and do it. It's your *job.* You can't let an employee be passed over year after year and not tell him or her why. It's just shameful.

Employees have to get clear, direct feedback from their managers. How many evaluations have I read in which a female manager has omitted *the* most important information the employee desperately needs to be told? Often, ironically, this may be the one thing that all the senior staff knows: She's too emotional, she nitpicks her employees to death, she's snotty to her co-workers, she's too defensive, she's too nice and won't tell her employees when they screwed up, everything's a crisis with her… And the person who *should* be armed with this information is the one the manager is withholding it from! Most bosses are scaredy-cats—be different. Be a lioness.

But Be Very Gentle

When you do communicate negative feedback, use delicate and sensitive language and put it in neutral job-related terms. Explain why it affects their job performance. Human resources may be able to help you. When I had to communicate difficult feedback, I sometimes wrote it down and asked a senior human resources manager to read it to make sure it was clear, but not harsh. Most employees are extremely sensitive to negative feedback and can really be hurt, or even damaged, by it. Try to couch it in the context of self-improvement—that we're all trying to get better, and we all have performance issues we need to focus on. Emphasize how wrong it would be if the manager *didn't* bring up areas for improvement.

I try to use language such as "I would suggest…," "In my observation…," "It appears to me…," so I don't present myself as all-knowing. If the feedback is accurate, the employee probably suspects it and doesn't need to have his or her nose rubbed in it. And it's the employee's responsibility to act on the feedback; you can't force a change in behavior. If you present it as advice or a suggestion, it's empowering to the employee to understand that it's up to him or her to embrace the feedback and put it into action. Finally, I like to link the change in behavior to greater success and happiness on the job. Problems in job performance hinder the employee's ability to advance and are often quite frustrating.

Terminations and Layoffs Are Terrible

You'll probably have to fire employees from time to time, and while it's no fun, I found laying people off, or making them redundant, as they say in the U.K., to be the worst experience of my work life. Layoffs are nearly always the result of poor management, particularly when they follow a spate of hiring. And yet, managers are nearly always reluctant to acknowledge who's at fault. It's heartbreaking to tell employees that they no longer have a job through no fault of their own. At least, when you fire someone (assuming you do it correctly, with an organized process following a series of warnings, both verbal and written), he or she had a pretty good idea it might be coming and why. With a layoff, they've had no notice and no time to prepare mentally or financially. Occasionally, firing someone who's in the wrong job gives that person a chance to start a new life with better prospects. When you lay someone off, there's no such hopeful component, especially if the economy is tanking. Laying off a talented, loyal employee is just horrible.

Amazingly, many employees exhibit tremendous loyalty, even following redundancies or a downsizing. I've seen employees work incredibly hard, getting a company ready to be sold or closed, simply because they're productive, ethical, and want things done right. It's quite moving to work with a group of employees who've been given pink slips and observe their remarkable maturity and dedication.

The Management Partnership

As your management skills improve, you establish a powerful dynamic with your employees. As you learn how to draw an improved performance from your employees, they will flourish and respond positively as part of your team. In turn, you become a stronger manager and can work on more subtle and challenging performance issues. Yay! Everyone is getting better!

Management is an area where you can truly differentiate yourself. If you treat your employees respectfully, honestly, and with care, they will make you successful and teach you more than you can imagine. When you become an outstanding manager, the path ahead of you is wide open.

Work—Why You're Paid

I attended a talk by a local CEO who was notable for being one of the few female biotech CEOs in town. After a glowing introduction and considerable fanfare, the moderator asked her, "So, what do you attribute your considerable success to?" The CEO, an unusually modest person, said, "I… um… work really hard?" And did she ever. In addition to her long hours during normal times, her CFO told me later that, even when the CEO was undergoing chemotherapy for cancer, she hardly missed a day in the office.

Despite all we've said about relationships, networking, attitudes, and so forth, your success ultimately depends on the quality of your work. It's appropriate here to spend some time on that topic. Books have been written on nearly every aspect of business (and a few of them are actually good), therefore, you can explore more deeply the technical aspects of your job, but I'll mention some mistakes I observe over and over, made not only by women, but by men too, and even experienced executives. Here's another area where you can differentiate yourself!

PowerPoint Makes You Stupid

I've been horrified by the prevalence and negative influence of PowerPoint presentations in the business world. I've spent countless hours watching executives stare at dumbed-down slides with a minimum of real information, listening to the presenter actually read these slides to them, as though they were not only dimwitted, but illiterate. Don't let this be you.

First, make sure a slide deck is really the best way to communicate the substantive information you need to convey. Would a collated package of data schedules provide more information? Or should a written proposal be circulated before the meeting? What are you trying to achieve? If you hope to persuade or drive a decision, perhaps a verbal presentation with no visuals, so your audience can focus on you, would be more effective. Are you hoping to stimulate a group discussion? In my experience, business people are typically so lulled into submission during a PowerPoint presentation that they won't speak up until they're sure all the slides are exhausted. Unfortunately, some executives capitalize on this tendency because they don't want to be challenged or have a discussion transpire. How sad.

Since PowerPoint presentations are usually bad, it's best if you can avoid them altogether. If there's no getting around it, and often your management team will balk at the notion of trying anything else, don't use simplistic bullet-point slides. They give the appearance of summarizing more complete and detailed data, that *could* be made available, but lamentably it often turns out that the development of those self-evident bullet points was the extent of the work undertaken. *That's* embarrassing.

If you've done your homework and have a significant amount of marketing, financial or technical data to present, hand that out ahead of time, including some summary tables. Then you can review the summaries with the group, without having to pore over the entire data set. Don't forget to number all the pages in your handout and to welcome questions about all aspects of the data and presentation. That's how real information gets shared and assessed, and good decisions are made.

There are excellent ways to summarize quantitative information in order to assist your audience to quickly grasp the correct conclusions without a time-consuming individual analysis. I highly recommend Edward Tufte's books on this topic. It can be done graphically, or with a table, or other pictorial approaches. Summaries can sometimes be converted into one very good slide, which may take some time to present and analyze, but represents the crux of your presentation. Don't succumb to the rule of thumb that you should only spend two to three minutes on a slide. How foolish to think that every slide is as complex as every other! I suppose that if all your slides are of the bullet-point variety, and your audience has fallen asleep, the time to present each one only varies by how fast you read.

Keep in mind that your audience will walk away with only two or three points they understood and can retain from your presentation. Make sure you emphasize those points in simple and clear language, and keep the rest of the presentation to a minimum. One of my trainers told me to pretend my audience was made up of children and to formulate the two or three most important takeaways in simple language a kindergartner could understand.

Don't forget the smart trick of presenting controversial material to key stakeholders *before* the meeting. That way, you can get feedback beforehand, and the meeting won't get mired down in an uncontrolled discussion. Many boards of directors will say they want "no surprises," and it will reflect poorly on you if you present material that shocks someone and causes a big commotion. I try to have material that may be a bit unexpected—to keep it interesting—but you definitely don't want any "gotchas." If you're presenting something that contradicts another manager's previous presentation, take him aside beforehand, so he has an opportunity to assess the material and won't be caught off guard. You don't want to make someone look stupid in front of the group.

Get the Facts

You would assume all important business decisions are based on factual unbiased data, but unfortunately, sometimes because of lack of information, significant decisions are made based on a powerful executive's opinion or "gut feel." Don't fall into this trap. Do your homework, seek input from others who may not share your viewpoint, challenge your own conclusions, and make sure you've done a good job analyzing as much quantitative data as you can gather. In some fields and industries, it's not easy, but you should try as hard as you can. Sometimes management teams deliberately avoid gathering unbiased data, particularly those related to their competition, because they've engaged in group-think, and they don't want their consensus to be challenged. Be different. Get the facts, analyze them open-mindedly, and present them fairly. Your company will benefit enormously from your objectivity.

Unfortunately, the "go with your gut" mentality tends to get worse as you rise in the ranks because executives rely more and more on their intuition as they gain experience. Because they've made good decisions in the past, they start to believe they're incredibly clever and forget that their previous good decisions were based on smart analysis, an open mind, and a more humble attitude.

Too often, I've seen business people—men and women—rely on the appearance of substance rather than going to the effort of developing, studying, or understanding what would support this appearance. This is similar to the PowerPoint slide presented as though it's a summary of substantive work when, in fact, the creation of the simple slide was the only effort the executive put in. The audience doesn't realize this because no one asks the hard questions that would draw out the data needed to support the slide. Too often, there's a preoccupation with a "professional" appearance rather than substance. Men may judge other men by whether or not they wear monogrammed shirts or by the car they drive. Women may judge other women by their clothes. Make sure you're not this silly and that you test for real quality and substance in your work and in the work of others.

Focus on the Big Picture

I'm sometimes surprised to see board members nitpick about unimportant issues, such as how many receptionists a company employs, while allowing enormously important decisions about acquisitions, new facilities, or overseas operations to be made without extensive debate. It seems to be human nature to gravitate toward smaller issues, that are more easily debated and where the stakes are low.

Now that you're aware of this pitfall, try to keep in mind the importance of any issue you are currently devoting effort to. You won't be working on significant strategic issues every hour of every day, but make sure your activities support and are important to the overall strategy of the company. Constantly assess the priority of the tasks in front of you and your staff in the current environment; what was important yesterday may not be today. Keep a running monitor in your head at all times of where your company is in its development and what the key initiatives are. What *has* to happen in the next six months? Is that what you're working on? If not, reassess how much time you're spending on alternate activities. If you haven't been told what has to happen in the next six months, ask. If no one can give you an answer, you better figure it out, even if it only pertains to your department or to you.

Work Toward the Bottom Line

Unless you work for a non-profit, your business is making, or is planning to make, money. Your investors are depending on you to turn a profit, and your priorities must be evaluated through this lens. Will your pet initiative decrease costs or increase revenue? If not, I'd reconsider it. Too many executives, particularly if they find themselves sidelined into unimportant departments or divisions, make the mistake of dedicating themselves to some project or system that may be interesting, but doesn't contribute to the company's bottom line. When this is recognized, it's not going to be perceived as important, and neither is its champion.

In particular, be honest with yourself about whether what you're working on is important to your company, or to you as you build your career. It's distasteful to spend your efforts on projects that augment your resumé but aren't critical to your company. Even if your manager doesn't call you on this abuse of company resources, you should reconsider and take up something else. Ultimately, other managers will notice, even if they say nothing, and your reputation will be damaged. Be sure your days are filled with activities that improve the financial value of your company. They don't necessarily need to have a direct impact on sales—they could be a cost reduction, an improved or more efficient quality system, or a better tool for currency hedges. Steer clear of projects that consume significant management time without a defined, quantified financial goal. Watch out for the mumbo jumbo and gobbledygook that seem to accompany pointless corporate-wide initiatives or bureaucratic processes that have no clear benefit. There are lots of fads in business. Work on something important.

Learn How to Run the Equipment

Doesn't it amaze you how many meetings start with ten minutes of wasted time as technical difficulties keep the meeting from starting? If we could save this time at all the meetings and presentations, in all boardrooms and conference rooms, across America, I can't imagine how much our GDP would go up. If you're working in a small company, make sure this *never* happens in any meeting you attend. Learn how to run the projector, the video and teleconferencing equipment, the screen, the lights, etc. If some new snafu happens, follow up every time so that it never happens again while you're in the room. It's usually not that hard; it's just that no one has bothered to learn it because "it's not their job." Assume it is your job. Make sure your company doesn't waste time on this kind of nonsense.

Learn how to run all the office equipment you routinely need, including the copier, fax machine, color printers, etc. Don't be the executive wandering in the hallway at 5:20 p.m., with a fax that MUST go out tonight, asking pathetically, "Has anyone seen Amber?" Ask nicely to be trained on the equipment by the administrative or IT staff. Acknowledge their expertise and ask for help. Usually, they're happy to share this information because they intelligently recognize that the company shouldn't become nonfunctional when they've taken a sick day or are late coming back from lunch.

Don't Avoid Work You Think Is Beneath You

Unfortunately, people in corporations are always on alert to detect any element of "prima donna" in a female executive. Don't give them any justification for this label. I sometimes see women back away from tasks they've been told are stereotypically female, as though somehow you'll wreck your career if you do them. I don't see it that way. Being useful and being able to do tasks others can't or won't do is quite empowering. The classic one that women react to is taking minutes at a meeting. A record of what was discussed, what decisions were made, and what the action items were is important and worth having. If the executive team wasn't in the habit of taking them, I volunteered. I write better and more quickly than many businessmen, and I'm a fast typist, so it was more efficient for me to do them.

More importantly, having control of the minutes gives you considerable power (which is a good thing—more about that soon). Of course, you won't include anything inaccurate, but if someone has made an important point or raised an important question, you can make sure it doesn't get lost. If the team has fallen into the habit of "meeting for meeting sake," you can use the minutes as a catalyst for action. If someone has a tendency to "forget" to do what has been assigned to him, you can include these to-do's in the minutes and provide them as a reminder.

The other classic lightning-rod task is making coffee. At the risk of infuriating someone out there, but since I'm sharing *all* my secrets, I'll just say that when I joined a new company, one of the first things I would do is ask my administrative assistant to show me how to make coffee. I'll let you think about all the messages I was sending by doing that. There are five.* Invariably, I was told that I was the first executive to ever ask.

Somehow, junior male employees seem to intuitively understand that doing a favor for someone in authority or pitching in to do menial work to impress their superiors helps their careers. Female employees sometimes hesitate or are worried it will send the wrong message. If you're smart, it can send absolutely the right message.

At the end of one summer early in my career, I offered to give a visiting executive a ride to the airport—on a Sunday—although that certainly wasn't part of my job. I wanted to talk to him one-on-one because he ran a European division I was interested in. It gave me a chance to hear about their activities and to show off my French. Sure enough, when he offered me a transfer to his division that fall, it paid off in spades. And on New Year's Eve, I was boarding a plane to go to my new job in Brussels!

**The Five Messages: 1) I am not a prima donna; 2) I don't expect you to wait on me; 3) I want to help you; 4) I'm different from other executives; 5) I like coffee!*

CHAPTER NINE

The Executive Woman's Dilemma

EXECUTIVE WOMEN FACE A NUMBER of dilemmas when they are working in a man's world. They start by learning, studying, and practicing effective behaviors to become good managers and contribute meaningfully to their corporation. They mimic successful men they work with and put the feedback they receive from their male managers into action. Here's where things can go haywire. Those behaviors are not usually associated with women and are more often perceived to be stereotypically male. This gender-bending can alarm the executive woman's co-workers and cause them to view her with suspicion and dislike. And you know, as well as I, what kind of name-calling ensues.

How is an executive woman supposed to exert influence and be an active member of the team without unleashing a backlash of disapproval and opposition upon herself? The answer is *"very carefully,"* and this chapter describes how. We'll look at how to speak up and be heard, without provoking a negative reaction. There are ways through this thicket, but it requires courage, common sense, and a delicate touch. In fact, you can learn to combine all your capabilities, innate or acquired, to evolve into an exceptional executive, one who really stands out from the crowd.

What? I Can't Hear You...

Since men think women aren't too smart and talk too much, it can be a real challenge for you to be heard. But, in order for you to contribute, you have to find a way for your ideas to resonate with your team. You can't advance in your career if you only listen and don't actively participate.

Your Moment to Shine

Most of the time you're listening, learning, and keeping your mouth shut. However, there will come a golden moment when a guy pauses to gather his thoughts, and you have a brief opportunity to speak. Don't waste it. Don't yammer on pointlessly; don't repeat what he said (that's not useful, is it?). Yet I frequently hear this kind of verbalizing from women—don't just reiterate his view. If you agree, nod and say, "I agree."

If you *don't* agree, if you know something he should know, or if you have something valuable to share, here's your moment to strike and make a difference. Now you can earn your salary! You can have a huge influence at moments like this. You can get someone hired, get a budget adjusted, get investment monies, change the strategy of an entire company, and move a mountain—all in that little moment while he pauses for breath.

So, when your time comes, here's your strategy: First, acknowledge what he said, and stay on topic. Then contribute something meaningful. Make sure he understands you. Be specific and clear. He's not an idiot. If it's useful, he'll pick up on it. He knows you've heard him out. He's convinced you have an open mind. He knows you'll be objective. If you're telling him that others don't agree with his view, he's in a position to hear why. If you're providing information that affects the viability of his plan, he'll want to hear that. If you're telling him who's backing an idea and why, he'll be all ears. If you have a good idea, let it out—he's ready.

Since you don't have much time, use it efficiently. You can't beat about the bush or present all sides of the argument—something I sometimes hear junior people struggle with. Say, "Here's what I recommend..." and then recommend it. You have to commit. Don't just express sympathy. Make specific suggestions, such as "Gee, it's disappointing we've gotten to this stage, but we need to pull it back from getting worse. What would you think about calling so-and-so and..." Or "That's sticky. How about if I get together with..." You need his approval (if he's the boss), but if you have recommendations and suggestions, they'll be helpful to him. If he doesn't respond, he might need time to think about it. In that case, you can add, "Well, think about it. The reason I think it might work is..." Remember, you may know more about the players than he does. That's just the nature of the role you've learned to play and his position in the organization.

This is the magic moment when you can be heard. It's important if you're talking to a decision-maker. It's even more critical if you're talking to someone who *talks* to a decision-maker. Usually it's hard for your voice to be heard several layers above you in the organization. You need someone who will carry your voice forward, who has access to the right people, and who has understood your idea and adopted it as his own.

Speak Up!

Group meetings are another place to voice your opinion—and you must take advantage of them. You can't sit silently and command respect. Again, your contributions should be brief, but in any meeting, there's usually at least one occasion when you should offer an idea, a suggestion, an explanation, etc. If you don't speak often, everyone in the room will perk up and listen when you do. Your words will carry more weight if you use them sparingly.

What you say should be relevant and important. If the meeting is headed in the right direction and the correct decisions are being made, perhaps you don't need to say anything. But if everyone in the room has lost their critical-thinking cap, and the discussion is becoming increasingly foolish, you must intervene. That's how you earn your keep.

You are a full-grown legitimate employee, and you have an opinion that deserves to be heard. If it's different from the others, then it's especially important that it be heard. Be courageous and speak up! I know it can be intimidating, but it gets easier. You'll be amazed at the impact you can have. Sometimes others in the room immediately express support for your comment because they were thinking the same thing but were afraid to say so.

I used to err on the side of being too quiet in meetings. I found it easier to provide my input off-line and use others as my mouthpiece. It was partially effective, but it wasn't enough. When I served on an all-male committee (well, except for me), the senior executive who chaired the meetings came to see me one day. After a long conversation about work, his background, and other seemingly unrelated topics, he finally said, "I need to tell you something."

"What?" I asked.

He said gently, "I sit in meetings with you, and I look at you, and I wonder what you're thinking."

Wasn't that a graceful way to tell me I had a bad, lazy habit? It's true. If you sit silently in a meeting, people wonder what's going on inside your head. You're clearly listening and mulling things over. They want to know: What are your conclusions? This excellent early tip taught me that I needed to be an active player in meetings. It was hard at first—I was nervous and worried about saying the wrong thing, *especially* when I was making comments that went against the consensus. But I practiced and practiced, just as you will, and I got better at it. I tried to think of it as something I *had* to do. And I felt good that even if my idea wasn't the one selected, I was contributing independently and genuinely to the discussion and that the decisions we made were stronger after that process.

It's Your Job

This trick of thinking of a challenge as just part of your job can overcome a lot of fear. I suffered from terrible stage fright at the beginning of my career, and I was nearly physically ill the first time I was sent to headquarters to give our annual budget presentation. I was very worried I would let my division down, and we wouldn't get the numbers we needed. I was sitting in the bathtub the night before, unable to relax, staring at the faucets, when I suddenly snapped and thought, "Oh, for *heaven's sake*. Get out there and do it. It's your *job*." And I did.

A local, respected attorney once said to me, "You know, I'm not that tough in my regular life. That's just not who I am, but I can be when I think my clients are being threatened. It's my job to protect them, so I can be quite fierce." If it's just one of your responsibilities, it's less about *you,* which makes it easier.

Voice Lessons

Let's talk about your instrument for being heard—your voice. You must understand and build it as part of your professional development. What kind of voice do you have? Do people mention they can always hear you down the hall? Tone it down. Are people always asking you to repeat what you said? Do your friends kid you about your "tiny little voice?" Pay attention to this important feedback.

With women, it's usually that they aren't loud enough. When women speak in meetings, they almost invariably speak too softly.

And if guys can't hear you, they'll blow you off. It's also irritating to see someone mouthing words across the room—or worse—speaking inaudibly to the leader of the meeting and leaving everyone else out. If you have a volume problem and can't seem to be audible, even when you try, consider seeing a vocal coach. Most voice teachers understand the dynamics of pitch and volume in public speaking, as well as in singing, and can help you make significant progress in a few lessons.

Here are some tips in the meantime. First, start with enough air. Sometimes women don't take a breath before they start talking. They start off with a minimum amount of air, let it all out in a rush, then start gasping for breath halfway through their sentence. I've seen women physically clutch as they run out of air, gulp, and snap their mouths shut when they can't go on. Guess what—it's hard to hear what you're saying with all that going on.

Poor speakers also hold their bodies rigidly and freeze their neck and throat muscles which contributes to a small and tinny voice. Don't fill up your lungs with air and refuse to let it out. Don't hold your stomach in. Nervousness is usually the culprit behind these bad habits, but you can counteract its effect by taking deep breaths and relaxing your body. And you might lose some of your nervousness in the meantime!

When you prepare to speak, straighten your back and let your tummy hang out. Relax your neck and jaw muscles; let your head rock a little on your neck to get rid of any tension. Take a good stock of air, and be sure your diaphragm is solid and compressed. Your tummy should feel loose, relaxed and flexible. Imagine that your tummy has a mouth and something to say, so it needs lots of room and exposure to be seen and heard.

As you speak, use lots of air. Don't worry about running out—there's more where that came from! Push your voice out and away from your body. Imagine you're throwing your voice across the room and banging it off the back wall. You don't have to shout to be heard. Go for a resonant and warm tone. Don't try to control the pitch or breathiness of your voice. Just speak naturally. Everyone's voice is different; if you don't distort your own voice by seeking an unnatural effect, it will emerge as a lovely and unique instrument.

Some women raise the pitch of their voice when they're trying to be heard. That creates a poor impression because it sounds strained and even shrill. Deeper tones carry farther (think of a foghorn), so try to keep your pitch natural and instead increase resonance and power to project your voice.

Another common mistake is to distort your natural voice by holding your jaw muscles rigidly and not opening your mouth enough. Watch professional speakers, like TV commentators—notice how wide they open their mouths. It shouldn't look artificial, like a choirboy who has been told to open his mouth. Start by unhinging your jaw, and letting it fall open to find your natural starting position. As you speak, the jaw will come up naturally and open and close appropriately for the vowels and consonants you're using. You shouldn't be "chewing" or gritting your teeth. Practice in front of a mirror until you can feel the difference between how you hold your mouth when you're telling a joke to your friends in a noisy restaurant and how you hold it when you're "on display" and speaking to an audience. Then practice using your relaxed, loud voice in meetings.

Remember to keep taking breaths as you talk. Don't rush your words and talk too fast. People need time to understand what you're saying. You can pause mid-sentence for effect and take a breath. Keep the floor with your body language and by the importance of what you're saying. Don't talk for too long, and conclude gracefully so other participants know when you're finished. Don't start repeating yourself as though you don't know how to stop talking and instead begin "petering out." That will cause others to start talking over you because they can see that you're effectively done. An awkward conclusion weakens your message.

Other Sistas' Voices

If another woman in the group is whispering and can't be heard, don't let her voice be ignored. Ask her to speak up. Get her to face the group and repeat her comments. Smile at her, and make room for her in the discussion. Don't let people get in the habit of ignoring women in meetings. If necessary, you can repeat what she said or incorporate her point into your comments. This will let her know her contributions are important and will help her gather the courage to speak again and maybe more loudly next time.

Still Not Being Heard...

Women frequently complain that when a woman makes a point, everyone ignores her, but when a *man* makes the same point a few minutes later, everyone agrees it's a great idea. This makes women mad as heck. I think there may be other factors in play here besides just gender, so be cautious before you conclude your co-workers are a bunch of chauvinists. First, the group may need time to think things through and have a concept sink in. Sometimes they need to hear it twice before they really get it. Sometimes the woman's presentation of the idea *was* a bit weak, or garbled, or too soft. Maybe it provoked some half-listening guy in the room to "have an idea." Having someone reiterate and reinforce your ideas can be quite helpful. Sometimes ideas develop on the fly, and it may sound like your idea, but it's really more of a modification of what you said. Or the group needed to hear it couched in slightly different terms. Glom on if you want to, and say, "Yeah! That's what I was trying to say. I think that's a great idea." The point is you're trying to move the company forward, not get credit for every little idea you have.

I know it's hard to take the high road here, but be generous. If you had a great idea but didn't get credit for it, be pleased it got carried forward. It's a compliment for someone to present one of your ideas as his own. That means it's worth something. It's also a whole lot better than being ignored. If a guy gets the credit for one of your ideas, take note of how you tried to communicate it. Maybe your tactic wasn't effective, so think about how you can do better next time. And don't worry that you'll never come up with another good idea. You're going to be full of good ideas!

Courage

In my observation, the single biggest factor that holds companies back is fear. Employees fear they'll lose their employment; managers fear being reprimanded; executives are fearful they'll make bad decisions; board members fear they'll be sued. This fear psychology can stymie an organization and thwart all other factors that would otherwise create a successful company.

Most employees are terrified of losing their jobs, and they know (despite everything management says to the contrary) that if there's a layoff coming, the first names on the list are going to be troublemakers, low-performers, or anyone who looks like a risk. No wonder most employees act like cheerleaders or yes-men. They won't ask questions at company meetings; they won't question the status quo; they won't make suggestions that might offend anyone; they won't speak out against injustice. And, if they're unhappy, they prefer to leave rather than fix the company they're in. The more limited their employment options are, the more likely they are to toe the line and go with the flow.

I once worked for a company that was the only major employer for fifty miles in any direction. That company was more governed by fear than any other organization I've worked for, except one. And *that* one, although there were alternative employment opportunities, had a strong culture of longevity. Employees worked there for thirty years and then retired. As long as you kept your head down, you were almost guaranteed employment. It was a good company, but quite paternalistic—employees weren't change agents there.

Don't underestimate how cowed your employees are and how much they'll just nod their heads and go along with you, even when your company is doing something incredibly block-headed. One company I worked for launched a huge company-wide initiative called SucSess (watch out for initiatives that have to be misspelled). It wasn't clear what it was—it seemed to have something to do with change, but if they ever told us what or how we were supposed to change, I missed that memo. Nevertheless, a couple of hours into the huge launch meeting, managers were standing up and pledging their support for SucSess. I felt like yelling, "What the heck are you talking about?" But as a junior employee, I didn't say a word. Another company I worked for spent a million dollars developing a new logo. When the rollout team came to my site, the employees in the back of the room whispered to each other, "It looks just like the Cingular logo." But nobody told senior management.

Down with Fear

If your company exhibits these characteristics, you have a problem—you *need* your employees to participate with passion at every level. If everyone pretends that problems don't exist, you can't solve them in a timely manner, and ultimately your competition will take market share from you. Companies with employees who care, who take pride in their work, and who seek constant improvement will outperform those governed by fear and whose employees are just along for the ride. If you've ever played on a sports team, you've seen this firsthand.

What can you do to heal a fearful environment? First, set a good example. Don't just coast—get involved and speak out. Ask questions, listen carefully to the answers, and if they don't make sense, ask again. Asking questions may drive more change than you might think as your colleagues take note that you weren't fired and begin asking questions themselves. If you begin to lose your nerve, ask yourself "What's the worst that can happen?" You'll be fired? So what. If you've managed your career well, you're very employable. Who wants to work for a company where you get fired for asking questions anyway? Innovator Steve Jobs, who passed away this year, said, "Remembering that you are going to die is the best way I know to avoid the trap of thinking you have something to lose." He was a brave guy; let's try to be more like him.

No matter what level you are in the organization or what fear environment you find yourself in, you can use the strategies in this section so *you* are the leader who rises above this culture and presents a shining example for all employees to break the fear mentality.

Maybe you're afraid you'll make someone mad—very understandable. Questioning the status quo does upset a lot of people who *should* appreciate it when someone is willing to stick her neck out. Practice and expand strategies in this chapter to emphasize the positive nature of your question or suggestion and downplay any adversarial or "gotcha" aspects to your comments. Often, women are very skilled at this because they've been practicing non-confrontational communication strategies their whole lives. They may be much better at this than men who are accustomed to a "if I'm up, you're down" dynamic to a relationship and who see every conversation as a competition. From that perspective, women are the perfect change agents in a fearful environment because they can move companies in the right direction in a non-threatening, positive manner.

Super-Courageous

But let's be realistic here: Women are in a very tough spot when it comes to speaking out publicly in an organization. We've already discussed that most businessmen think women talk too much. In addition, most men hate being corrected or put down by a woman. Bringing up an uncomfortable or unpopular point is a very fast way to unleash a flood of criticism. How can you navigate this difficult dilemma? You know you have to speak up to perform your job correctly, and you know that's a behavior you'll probably be punished for. It's daunting. When faced with this "damned if you do, damned if you don't" quandary, many women decide to leave the whole issue behind and go off to take care of their kids, start their own business, or do anything else besides work in this crazy place.

I already said you have to be courageous—now you have to be super-courageous! If you know you're likely to be attacked, you can prepare yourself, do your best to ward off adversity, and protect yourself so you don't lose your nerve. Remind yourself that what you're doing is truly amazing. Many women falter here, so in the beginning, keep your expectations low. You'll get better with practice and in time, will find it less nerve-wracking.

Your Evil Twin

Because women know that they're caught in the cross-hairs of these negative attitudes, they are sometimes very uncomfortable at work and can in turn be quite difficult to work with. This is a nasty trap that executive women sometimes fall into because of fear and a lack of confidence in their abilities. Before we talk about what you should do, let's talk about how you *don't* want to come across. Imagine a hyper-intense, grim, uptight, paranoid colleague who takes everything the wrong way. She's ready to pull herself up in outrage at every imagined slight. She's stiff, hostile, and carries a giant chip on her shoulder. She's insecure about her competence, so she doesn't ask or answer questions, over-uses lingo in an attempt to fit in, and hides behind inauthentic emails and overly-formal presentations. She barricades herself in her office and discourages drop-in visits. Wow. I bet you want to build a relationship with her, right? Have you worked with someone like her? You can use her as the polar opposite of how you want to behave.

Use Preambles, Not Hedges, as Effective Lead-Ins

Let's define some terms here and distinguish between a *lead-in,* a *hedge,* and a *preamble.* Many women use a *lead-in* when they want to make a point. They've learned to do this since they were in elementary school, and in my opinion, it can be very useful if it's honest and carries a positive message. Since women are harshly judged when they speak out, they've learned to do so in the "nicest" way possible. They use lead-ins like, "Honey, I was wondering if you would..." or "I know you don't like it when I nag, but..." or "Could I make a suggestion?" But there are good lead-ins and bad lead-ins. Some lead-ins are effective because they imply the speaker is on the other guy's side and get him to lower his guard. Some are terrible and denigrate the speaker or insult the other guy in an underhanded, mean way. And some are just words filling the air for no reason because the speaker is afraid to get to the point.

A *hedge* is a lead-in whereby the speaker tries to take the sting out of her point by downplaying her intelligence, pointing out she probably doesn't know what she's talking about, or that this might be a stupid idea. This style has been described as stereotypically female, but it's also Midwestern. Lots of men where I come from talk like this. It's a way to gracefully allow the person you're talking with to disagree with you without provoking a confrontation. It can be quite a dance.

> Midwestern Guy #1: *Well, here's how I see it—and I probably don't know anything about what I'm talking about—but I think they're*

taking advantage of you, and you need to tell them you can't work that much overtime.

Midwestern Guy #2: *No, no, I know. I know. You make a valid point.*

Midwestern Guy #1: *Like I say, I probably don't know anything about your situation.*

Midwestern Guy #2: *No, I appreciate you bringing that up. The thing is—this phase we're going through right now? I think it's temporary, and I don't want to say anything 'cause I know Paul can't do nothin' about it right now. I just gotta keep on keepin' on 'til we get through this.*

Midwestern Guy #1: *Well, like I say, I probably can't see the whole picture from where I sit.*

Midwestern Guy #2: *No, no. You're right. This is a very tough situation.*

This could go on for hours. Here's how a couple of New Yorkers would do it.

New York Guy #1: *Wassa matta witchu? You tell them to take that overtime and shove it.*

New York Guy #2: *You talkin' to me? Huh? Oh my god. You don't have a clue. Whatever.*

New York Guy #1: *Oh yeah? Oh yeah? You're just chicken.* [clucks]

New York Guy #2: *Shut the f*** up! You don't even know.*

You want to aim for somewhere between these two styles. Don't use hedges that detract from your message like, "This probably won't work..." or "I'm new here, but..." or "This might sound silly..." These lead-ins make the listener wonder why the speaker is saying anything if what follows won't work, or is silly, or comes from a person who has nothing to offer because she's new.

You can, however, use lead-ins that set the stage for what follows in a positive, non-threatening way. Let's call those *preambles,* and they're a good tool. I hesitate to offer specific sentences or phrases because your body language and intonation carry more of your "message" than the actual words, but I recognize you need examples to help formulate your own. Beware of sounding stuffy as though you're reading something someone has told you to say, or using clichés in a false attempt to cushion your message ("I hear what you're saying, but..."). Try to sound natural and genuine. Positive, effective preambles could be: "Could I ask a question?" or "Here's something we tried at one company I worked at..." or "I have an idea. See what you think of this..." or "I like where we're going with this. What about..." These preambles convey "where you're coming from," and help others hear your message with a non-defensive, open attitude. Good preambles reflect candor, humility, and a team spirit.

Other Tactics

Here are other suggestions for different ways you can speak out, what approaches you might try, and how to avoid the pitfalls associated with being an "uppity" woman.

- **Be Honest**

  This is solid advice in nearly every aspect of business, in communicating, managing, negotiating, and questioning. People often can tell if you're speaking authentically or playing games. Don't toy with people. Put yourself out there in a forthright way. It breeds tremendous trust and can take the tension out of a situation if your colleagues see you're a straight shooter. Also, if you conduct yourself honestly, it keeps things simple for you internally, and you don't have to worry about being a phony. Mark Twain said, "If you tell the truth, you don't have to remember anything."

If you don't understand why an initiative is being proposed and its value is unclear to you, say so. You might say, "I was thinking about this problem differently..." because you were. That's an honest starting place. You could try, "Please don't interpret my question as implying I *don't* think this initiative has value—I just don't understand it. What are its intended consequences?" If you're just gathering information, you can emphasize that this is part of your assessment process; it doesn't mean you're opposed to the proposal. And if you discover you'd previously missed a key point that clears up your misunderstanding, acknowledge that. Don't leave the team wondering if you're now convinced or not. For honest communication, your team members need to know that when you've made a mistake in comprehension, you'll admit it.

Ask Questions

If you're doubtful that a proposed timeline is realistic, ask, "What will need to happen for this timeline to be met?" The ensuing discussion will allow you to determine if it seems do-able or overly optimistic. If you have doubts, others in the room probably do too. This may permit a more open discussion where obstacles can be addressed, rather than avoided, as often happens in a fearful environment in which everyone has doubts, but no one will bring them up.

Speak as a Team Member

If you're concerned about unforeseen expenses, say, "I know all of us are concerned about cost, so I would like to know how this will fit into the budget." Make sure your body language, tone of voice, and language choices are all positive, non-threatening, and non-defensive. Your comments should come from the perspective of a team member working collaboratively to solve problems. Keep the rest of the group on your side, and don't set up a "you versus me" tone.

Don't Send Mixed Messages

Be conscious of your body language and intonation, as these send messages along with what comes out of your mouth. Don't giggle if you're trying to make a serious point. Don't carry a hostile tone if you're trying to be persuasive. Usually, these confusing signals are a sign of stress, so try to relax as you communicate. It will help bring all your messages together in a positive, powerful package.

Be Modest

Recognize that you're only one member of a group, and although your opinion is important, it isn't the only one. Your suggestions may not prevail, and that's not the end of the world. Your job is to make sure all the facts are in and to speak out and state your position. It's not to have your way all the time. Don't get stubborn and restate your opinion over and over. Your words will have more impact if they're few and concise. Concede with grace; if your position truly is far away from the rest of the group, you're unlikely to have much impact by arguing. Let it go. There will be other opportunities to move the company closer to perfection.

Keep the Big Picture in Mind

Be selective about what issues you raise and make sure they're important. You don't want to nitpick about every little shortcoming in the company. People will stop listening to you if you object to everything. Ask yourself, does it matter? If yes, speak up; if no, drop it. If the right thing is being done for the wrong reason, keep quiet and get on with more important issues. Too much meeting time is spent with participants quibbling over details or glomming onto someone else's comments. Try to keep your airtime short—make sure the topics you raise are important and you get to the point fast.

✦ Suggest Alternatives

If you have reservations about a proposal or current practice, put your critical-thinking cap on and come up with a superior alternative. You can't just throw stones all the time. Sometimes you'll discover that, although the proposal isn't great, it's actually the best alternative.

✦ Don't Play Devil's Advocate

The more experience I have, the more I feel this is pointless. Debating issues brought up by "the devil's advocate" can be a real time-waster. Sometimes employees use this phrase when they have a concern, but they're afraid to say so. Sometimes men say this to a woman in order to get some airtime, see if they can get a rise out of her, or because they don't want to challenge her directly. I would avoid using this term and instead try to get people who say this to state their position. "Playing devil's advocate" sounds as if someone is pretending to play a role. Make your colleagues take real positions by asking if they have a genuine concern. If you get them to be straight with you, a meaningful discussion can occur. If they admit they were just fooling around, the group can move onto more productive activities.

✦ Don't Use Clichés

The term "business clichés" is almost a cliché in itself because so many people make fun of them. Lucy Kellaway has skewered a number in her hilarious column for *The Financial Times*: "reach out," "going forward," "uphold our values." Please don't say "give 110 percent"—that's nonsensical. Some business people use words in a peculiar way because they sound fancy—monetize, enthuse, innovate a paradigm shift—when simpler words would be more clear. Don't hide behind clichés as a lazy way to throw lingo around without offering anything new; what do "making a difference," "value-added," or "world-class" really mean? When you describe concepts in your own words, rather than using vague or meaningless catch-phrases, you communicate more clearly. Don't be like cartoonist Roz Chast's superhero *Idiotman* who says, "At the end of the day, it is what it is!"

Note that I'm not talking here about idioms or expressions. Idioms can be lively, expressive, and a wonderful shorthand to communicate a concept in a subtle or humorous way, such as "Little pitchers have big ears," or "Three people can keep a secret, if two of them are dead."

Writer Martin Amis noted, "All writing is a campaign against clichés, not just clichés of the pen, but clichés of the mind and clichés of the heart." And so it is with you when you speak; you want to use words that mean something, that express your unique idea in a fresh and energetic way, not words that are over-used, boring, or stupid.

✦ Ask Again

If your comment is ignored, don't be afraid to bring up your point again. Sometimes your first explanation wasn't clear enough, and other team members have to hear it again. Certain complicated points need time to sink in. If no one picks up on your point, don't be shy and fade away like a shrinking violet. Be nice about it when you bring it up again, but you can say, "At the risk of being a bore, I just want to mention again my concern that..." Or, "You know, I didn't get any feedback on my question from the other day, but I would be interested in discussing the issue of..." You'll be able to tell if people understood your idea and were deliberately ignoring it (and maybe you can now figure out why), or if they didn't understand it, or if they're now ready to discuss it. But you have to be courageous enough to ask again.

Keep It Light

Try to stay loose. If no one's going to die, don't get too intense. Business is serious, but it's not life itself. Try to keep everyone involved, but not uncomfortable and defensive. No good discussion results from that atmosphere, and usually individuals are so distracted by the emotional heat of that kind of conversation that they can't participate effectively. Emphasize you're not personally invested in the issue, and demonstrate that by your tone and non-partisan participation in the discussion. Sometimes it's effective to restate someone else's position and say, "I see your point," assuming you do. It demonstrates that you're a democratic participant in the discussion and you're not trying to "win." The objective is to arrive at the best decision for the company regardless of whose idea it is and who has lined up on which side. As you and your team get good at it, you'll find that other executives catch on and participate honestly and productively, sharing their disapproval or support of multiple aspects of a topic, instead of taking sides and fighting.

Hanging Tough

What if someone gets mad? Some people are always ready for a confrontation; they come into work in the morning looking for an altercation. Sometimes, no matter how skillfully you handle the discussion of a sensitive topic, someone gets upset. If you feel as though you mishandled your side of the discussion, or if your motives were misinterpreted, you can seek out your agitated colleague after he has had time to cool off. You can apologize in private and explain what you wish you'd said better. You can gain huge points and win a tremendous ally with this kind of humble and honest behavior. On the other hand, if someone went off irrationally and inexplicably, I'd suggest you let it go, so he isn't forced to apologize for his behavior. That might make him mad all over again. Try to treat everyone on the team with the same respect, deference, and courtesy without kowtowing to the person with the biggest temper.

While we're at it, don't let bullies bully you into keeping quiet. You still have a job to do. If they yell at you, get tough and brush it off. That they yell is their problem; how you react to it is *your* problem, and you're in control of that. Obviously, it doesn't make for a very productive discussion if they get mad and yell, but that's not your fault. I had a boss who used to say, "Who's the bigger idiot—the idiot or the guy arguing with the idiot?" If you've followed all the suggestions in this chapter, you've done your job well, and you can afford to ignore a bully.

Don't get upset if you get interrupted. This can be a sign of disrespect and certainly is, if an overbearing person in the room constantly interrupts you to keep you from making your point. Once you begin to notice this, it can really get under your skin, so don't fall into that trap. Accept that many people are threatened by you and they're trying to cope with that fear and their own insecurities. You may need to double up on your opening non-threatening preambles, specifically ask for the floor again if your point was lost, and smile and say, "I'm glad we're all interested in talking about this." Sometimes people do interrupt you without meaning to be disrespectful. There are different discussion styles, and some people don't wait for a moment of silence before they jump in.

For your part, be sure that when your comment is finished, you stop talking. Some people begin to reiterate their comments if they haven't been interrupted, which encourages others in the group to jump in and start talking over them. Group discussions can get pretty wild, and there's often a lot going on at once. As you train yourself to be observant of group dynamics and learn how to gracefully insert yourself in the discussion, make your point, and then return to listening, you'll enjoy the action and even find it fascinating. Remember not to get your feelings hurt and hang in there!

Public Versus Private Statements

Make sure your private comments are consistent with your public ones. Don't be supportive or silent about a proposal in a meeting, and then complain about it behind closed doors to someone else. Reiterate your concerns (if you have any) in a manner consistent with the approach you took in the meeting: It's not personal; it's our job to ask questions; I need to understand this; I'm on the team, and I want to do a good job; I want my company to succeed. Repeating your message in different contexts will clarify it and convince others that it's legitimate and should be taken seriously.

That being said, sometimes it's better to raise your concerns in private. Speaking privately with a colleague is less likely to be perceived as a threat or to provoke an angry reaction. It's appropriate to speak privately when there's a sole decision maker you need to influence, to avoid forcing someone to lose face in public, or when there are political considerations that shouldn't be broadcast in an open forum. If a surprising decision is announced that you should have been consulted about and weren't, you should object to this in private and emphasize that the correct process shouldn't be circumvented in the future. Although you've done little to change a fearful environment if no one has seen you speak out, it's still better to speak out in private than not at all.

And finally, sometimes you have to get someone else to carry your message for you. It would be better if you could present your views openly and hope your reputation for fairness and objectivity would allow them to be heard without prejudice, but sometimes that's just asking too much of the circumstances. Perhaps the appearance of a vested interest is so powerful, you think no one will believe you're being impartial. In that case, you would want to approach a colleague who might share your view to see if he or she would be willing to speak for you.

Common Sense

Let's talk about common sense because it turns out not to be that common. When you contemplate issues confronting your company, you will bring to bear your education, experience, analytical skills, wisdom—in short, all your intellectual capabilities. Be sure you don't leave your common sense at home. Too often, I see mistakes made in the business world that when considered retrospectively are clearly ludicrous. "How could this have happened?" we ask ourselves. Unfortunately, it's all too easy for foolish thinking to prevail when big egos are combined with high aspirations and financial pressure. Keep your skeptical spectacles and critical-thinking cap close at hand, and make sure you apply common sense to the decisions you and your company make.

Avoid Fads

Be suspicious of "the latest thing" because these ideas *à la mode* are frequently later revealed to have been flawed. When *The Wall Street Journal* is talking about it, when your CEO played golf with someone who just implemented it, or when your Marketing Vice President just met someone on the plane who's selling it, be wary. Be sure you consider these fads in the context of your own company. For instance, when Irish subsidiaries were the rage, hundreds of companies opened them whether they were appropriate or not, and subsequently many regretted their decision. Centralizing, decentralizing—some companies go through so many cycles of each, it becomes a running joke. Merging, acquiring, divesting, off-shoring—all these trends seem to wax and wane without a valid business reason. If executives and boards of directors used more common sense, these expensive reorganizations and transactions would be fewer and more meaningful.

Be leery of something "everyone is doing." Are all your peers putting in a hugely complex, customized, and expensive computer system despite their very small size? They've been sold a bill of goods. Suppose someone tries to sell you a new hiring assessment tool and claims it will replace your trusted recruiter's twenty years of experience. Does that make sense? Be the smart one, and don't fall victim to someone's aggressive marketing campaign.

Why is the business world so prone to latch onto the latest fad? Sometimes I wonder if business people are just bored with trying to grow sales and turn a profit. They seem remarkably ready to spend inordinate amounts of time discussing and disseminating the latest hot thing. If you've ever had to read that business book about cheese (or was it that cheesy book about business?), you know what I'm talking about.

✦ Watch Out for What Seems Counter-Intuitive

Sometimes "new" business concepts are published that fly in the face of years of established management fundamentals and documented organizational behavior. It's not a good sign if tried-and-true business practices are now considered old-fashioned and are tossed out because of some bizarre new idea. Some of these ideas simply fall apart the minute you apply some common sense to them. Suddenly everyone is wearing the hat and citing the slogan without much critical discussion or peer review. If it seems counter-intuitive, don't forget that it just might be stupid. What if someone proposes a theory that you should just hire "good people," regardless of their abilities and your company's needs, and everything will work out fine? Is that rational?

If explanations seem overly complicated and come out with an illogical answer, make sure your team isn't engaging in group-think or a game of The Emperor's New Clothes in which no one wants to tell the CEO his latest idea is for the birds. It will be up to you to speak out and bring your common sense to bear on the topic.

Keep It Simple

Could you explain it to a child? Most business concepts are not that complicated, compared to other fields of study. You should be able to explain most important business changes in simple language and in a few sentences. If there's considerable "background" or "context," beware. Bad ideas and bad news are often presented with a morass of data, complicated explanations, overwhelmingly detailed slides, and confusing jargon. I used to say to my staff when they would run in my office with their hair on fire, "What happened? Use short words." Clear explanations are simple. The corollary is "Will this make sense to your employees?" If no, maybe that's because it's a bad idea.

- **Keep Personalities Out of It**

  Are initiatives or upheavals being driven by personalities, rather than rational arguments? I've seen huge reorganizations, expensive and dumb, undertaken simply to give the appearance of a promotion to a powerful executive. How disgraceful is that? Be alert to the power of the CEO's spouse. Make sure the company doesn't relocate its headquarters just because that's where she wants to live. Don't laugh. It happens all the time.

- **Follow the Incentives**

  Ask how vendors are compensated to understand what their incentives are before you adopt something new. Make sure you understand who stands to gain what when you're considering making a change. Figure out how everyone in a transaction is being paid whether they're bankers, brokers, attorneys, or agents. It will help you put their "advice" into proper perspective.

A Powerful Combination

Executives who regularly exercise courage and common sense are surprisingly rare and generally very successful. We've discussed courage and how you overcome fear to be able to speak out and contribute productively to your company. We've also given some examples to make sure that common sense prevails in your company. Now that you've learned about both, you'll be amazed at how successful you become.

Think for a minute about how special you are and what you bring to your company. You possess the natural capabilities you acquired as you were raised as a woman in our society, you're highly educated, and you've received extensive management training throughout your career. You've embraced feedback and practiced behaviors that didn't come easily to you. You've worked extremely hard to develop a wide array of skills. You keep your skeptical spectacles and your critical-thinking cap close by at all times. And you've read this book.

Now, you really are a lioness—strong, brave, and vocal. You are the rare executive who's willing to put your hand up and ask questions, get engaged, and push for what you think is right. You show real courage in being willing to stand apart from the group, to apply common sense to the issues at hand, and analyze business choices from your unique role in the organization. In the lingo of sports teams, you play your position.

Nevertheless, you're always on the side of the team; you recognize your opinion may not always be correct, and the team's decision is the one you'll support. Recognizing the value (and limitations) of your own decision-making ability, and learning how to unlock the *power* of a team, is the key to leadership. When you turn that key, you step into a new world—a fun, surprising, exciting, and fast-moving one. Join the party.

CHAPTER TEN

The Pride of the Lioness

YOU HAVE ACHIEVED GREATNESS and have overcome remarkable hurdles by moving into the executive ranks. This chapter celebrates your accomplishments but forewarns you about a few more last challenges you may face. Remember that you have achieved considerable visibility now, therefore, if you stumble, it will be public. That doesn't make your mistakes any worse—but it does mean you need to demonstrate superb confidence so that you're not undone by them and their aftermath. Hold onto all the skills and strengths that have brought you this far, and you'll do just fine. Because you have prepared yourself well, being successful at this senior level is no harder than at the other levels. Don't lose your head, use your staff wisely, and be brave.

Power and Risk

Some of the women I've worked with avoided using words related to power, such as, well, "power," or "authority," or "control."

Perhaps it's because people often view women with power negatively. Nevertheless, it's a useful way of describing roles and responsibilities to more junior employees, and I use it to explain how organizations work. You can clarify roles by saying, "I have the power to make that happen," or "You don't have the authority to make that decision." Women, in particular, need to consciously make sure they understand who has the power to do what in a corporation. Power not only means you get to make the decision; it means you *have* to make the decision. This needs to be spelled out and clearly assigned to a woman because, if she seems unsure and hesitates, some guy will likely step in to take over. This can be confusing to everyone and wreaks havoc with the organizational structure.

Power Is a Good Thing

One morning I was invited to a breakfast meeting at one of our local delis. When I walked into the restaurant at 7 a.m., I was thunderstruck. The place was *humming;* every table was full of people, and it's a big restaurant. There was talking and persuading, pitching and hustling, questioning and *selling*. You could practically hear cash registers ringing. There was *a lot* going on—and other than me and the waitresses—there were no women. There wasn't even a spouse. When I mentioned this phenomenon to a friend, she said, "Oh, you didn't know? That's where deals are done in this town." So much for having to go to the Men's Room. It's even open to the public.

There was so much power in that room it was almost explosive. And you can bet those guys weren't mincing their words about who has the power to do what. And why weren't there any women there? Because women don't have any power; no one needs to go to them or wants to go to them. I'm exaggerating, a bit, but let's be clear: power is a good thing—you should want it. Think of all the good things you'll do with it!

But with Power also Come Responsibility and Risk

As you rise in the organization and gain power, you're responsible for more employees, decisions, and outcomes, and that translates into stress. More is required of you, and that's why those big jobs pay more. Each new level requires greater skills. You have to become smarter, smoother, and speedier. What seemed hard for you at the beginning of your previous job is now pretty ingrained. But you have a whole new set of challenges you must handle without coming apart. You're now at a greater risk of failure than before.

The first time I made a fool of myself in public and made a big mistake on my company's quarterly analyst call, I pretended everything was fine for the rest of the day, and then I went home and stared at the wall for two hours. I was so *embarrassed*. That's one risk you run as you become more powerful and more visible: You might go down in flames—and everyone will know. Think carefully before you decide to move up to the executive level. It isn't for everyone. You have to be willing to stumble in public and be openly criticized. You must be tough enough to hold your head up and keep going. And you need enough self-confidence to tell yourself that you can gain the new skills you need to be successful in this position, just as you've done before. Eventually, I almost got used to making a fool of myself since I did it so often!

Making decisions is also risky. I sometimes suspected that a female co-worker veered away from the power that came with her position because she didn't want to risk making the wrong decision. But you can't sneak away from it. First, it's your job. Second, if you're best qualified to make the decision, it has to be you. You may discover with the clarity of hindsight that a decision you thought long and hard about was just wrong, but you can't sweat it. If you made a bad hire, signed a damaging deal, made a financial commitment you shouldn't have, don't fall apart. You did the best you could. Now, you have to decide what to do next. Every day you have to make decisions, and they don't ever stop.

I asked a smart corporate attorney who works with many female executives what differentiates the good ones from the not-so-good ones. "The good ones *take charge*," she said. She described how a CFO stepped up, pulled a team together, and laid out a plan of action after her company had been hit with some bad news. Her actions calmed the employees and showed them how the organization could move forward.

Don't shy away from power if you choose to keep moving up, but be aware that it comes with a price.

Leadership

Being a good leader is complicated and the subject of a multitude of books. I'll address some particular areas where inexperienced female executives may feel at a loss. The bad news is that you can get caught in the Executive Woman's Dilemma—you must demonstrate good leadership characteristics to be successful, but if you do, you run the risk of releasing a harsh backlash from misogynist factions. So be it. Forewarned is forearmed. Don't be surprised if a promotion into senior ranks generates some name-calling, and don't take it personally. It doesn't mean you're not a good leader. The good news is that you may already possess some very positive leadership capabilities you didn't know you had. That will make being a good leader easier than you thought. You may even discover you'll become a more natural and graceful leader in a corporate setting than your male peers.

What Is a Leader?

I found this concept somewhat mysterious when I was young, and perhaps you do, too. I had a mental picture of a remote, fierce figure who awed his followers with his strength and technical prowess. Many of our images of leadership are masculine, and even militaristic. "How can I ever develop into a leader?" I thought, "That's just not my style—a collaborator, partner, mentor, sure—but leader? That's a big word." Fortunately, an astute human resources colleague sent me for leadership training after I'd been a manager for a few years. If the concepts of leadership don't come to you intuitively, consider taking a similar course. You'll get to know yourself much better and gain a lot of confidence.

Even if you don't go for leadership training, you can replicate some of its benefits on your own. Your first task is to develop a profile of yourself. In my leadership training course, we completed about ten assessment tasks, including the Myers-Briggs, some surveys and self-assessments, staff evaluations, a 360° review which includes feedback from subordinates, peers, and supervisors, etc. Although each of these is limited on its own (I find it particularly galling that the corporate world has bought into the notion that four letters can describe your personality), but when all the feedback is taken together, you begin to form a picture of your natural strengths and weaknesses. Many of us commented that it was what our mothers or spouses had been telling us all along. This will help you identify areas you may need to work on, as you move into more important leadership roles. For example, you may discover you're very task-oriented and need to deliberately make a point to leave your office and move around the building to increase your visibility. Keep in mind that any adjustments you make will be modest. There's nothing wrong with you; you're just shoring up some weaker areas because you possess naturally strong talents in a different area. You're working on creating a well-rounded leader who can do it all.

Attitudes about corporate leadership have changed in the last two decades, and you can benefit from them. Previous expectations were that a corporate leader was a hard-driving warrior who led by domination and control, whereas a more modern view is that a good leader establishes a strong vision, builds consensus, and motivates employees to achieve the company's goals as a team. In other words, success is measured more in terms of "us," rather than "him." This may appeal to you because many women easily gravitate toward a more collaborative orientation to work and are uncomfortable with self-promotion. If that's more natural for you—great! You're already on your way to being a good leader.

Think about the following leadership qualities to see if they come naturally to you or not. I picked these out because I notice aspiring female executives are not always aware of their importance and may not devote as much time to developing them as they should.

Good Leaders Have a Vision and a Plan

Being a good leader means more than filling an important box on the organizational chart. We've spent considerable time defining the skills that make you an effective manager. Being a good leader in a corporate environment requires even more of you. You'll help set the direction of the company and inspire your employees to achieve your long-term goals. This vision needs to be supported by a practical and tangible plan that includes timelines, financial requirements, and tactical goals for your department heads. Of course, you won't do this alone. The vision and the plan need to be supported and contributed to by your board of directors and your staff, but you're the one to point to the star in the sky and say, "That's where we're going."

I occasionally see women stumble at this stage. Perhaps insecurities arise at this very high level or subtle undermining increases as a woman rises in an organization. Senior female executives may appear to forget some of the skills that made them successful and become more dictatorial at this stage of their career. Although it's tempting to feel as though this is when you have something to prove, now—more than ever—is when you must fully use your collaboration and team-building skills. You must emphasize the inclusive nature of building a vision and a plan and not cram them down everyone's throat. Take the time to build broad support.

Good Leaders Make Decisions

Because of the scrutiny and pressure that comes with more senior positions, some executives become paralyzed, particularly if they're pulled in different directions by very smart subordinates who know far more about their specific functions than our new leader does. It shouldn't become a popularity contest or a competition between managers to present their ideas in the most forceful way. New leaders, even strong ones, can feel uneasy or even intimidated under this intense pressure. Nevertheless, the role of the leader is to make decisions and to take the heat for them if they prove to be bad. Responsibility and accountability go with the salary and the perquisites. Here are a few tips to help you with the decision-making process:

- Take your time making a decision. Don't just make a decision to show how powerful you are. Get the relevant information and think it through. Talk to people. Understand the pros and cons. A rushed decision is unlikely to be a good one.
- Don't make a decision before you have to. How much time have you spent in meetings, listening to staff members argue and debate an issue that turns out to be moot? Don't spend time making decisions about hypothetical situations. If there's more information coming that will affect the decision, wait for it.
- Once you make a decision, don't keep reconsidering it. That's very frustrating to the employees. Announce the decision, the reasons for it, and move on.
- If a decision turns out to have been a bad one, learn from it, but don't let it keep you from making the next one. You'll be making *many* decisions, and not all of them will come

out well. One boss said to me, "As long as you're right more often than you're wrong, you're doing okay."

- *Make* a decision. Don't forget that's why you're paid a high salary. You have to commit yourself to being a good leader. Don't waffle or try to be all things to all people. It's your job to make decisions and take the blame or credit for them.

Good Leaders Are Likeable

This may surprise you because our old-fashioned view is that it's bad if people like you because it means you're soft and won't "drive the troops." On the contrary, effective leaders are well-liked in their companies, and people gravitate to them and enjoy their presence. Who knew? You may discover you already have great skills in this area because you network easily, you have good social skills, you're friendly, and people like you! Of course, you aren't trying to make friends with the employees; your relationships within the organization will always be appropriately professional. But just because it's a business relationship doesn't mean people can't like you.

Limo drivers and other service providers tell me that the more senior an executive is, the more likely he or she is to be kind, courteous, and understanding. It's the lower-ranking employees who are nasty and unsympathetic. Why not start building your leadership credentials by being nice to taxi drivers, delivery people, and waiters?

Good Leaders Are *Always* On

If you're at the top of an organization, you can never have an off-day. You can never slip and express a lack of confidence in what the team is doing. You can never complain about failure. You can never talk dispiritedly to your staff, even in confidence. It's your role to express faith in your mission and to motivate. Remember, it's not about you—it's about *them*.

Good Leaders Are Visible

It's important that employees see you and have a chance to assess your attitude about what's happening. They become extremely worried when you're not around, if you look worried, or if your habits change. You must be a constant positive presence and visibly demonstrate your conviction and high energy. There's no way around this: You have to leave your office and walk around and talk to people. Err on the side of doing this too frequently, and you'll probably get it closer to right than most. We all get busy, but this is extraordinarily important. If this doesn't come easily to you, just keep doing it; you'll get better at it. Note that you have to go into your employees' space; you can't just order them to come to you. They need to see you're interested in what they're doing. Take every excuse to walk around and see what's going on, in the warehouse, on the plant floor, in credit and collections, everywhere. Employees love to see you. It's a real morale-booster.

Good Leaders Bring Out the Best in Their Team

Being the leader doesn't mean you have all the answers yourself. You have to motivate your team to come up with great ideas, to collaboratively vet them, and work together to make the most of all the skills of each of your individual staff members. That's what makes managing people fun because the team accomplishments are greater than those that any one person could produce. It sometimes seems miraculous to watch a team collectively put their heads together and come up with superb results. Although it's a collaborative effort, it introduces an element of competition, so be careful to balance those tensions. All members should feel engaged and motivated to contribute their best effort. No one should be watching skeptically from the sidelines.

One of the exercises in my leadership course brought home to me rather bluntly this notion that leaders may not have all the answers.

Our assignment was to rank in priority order a list of supplies and tools taken on a hypothetical camping trip during which our car had broken down. We initially worked alone to establish a baseline of our own ideas. We then got together in small groups to come up with a consensus list. I volunteered to record the group's ideas on the board and organize our thinking. I quickly realized that one of the guys in the group had figured out how to survive the cold night and another had worked out a signaling system to make our whereabouts known. I also realized that my own priority list was useless because I hadn't thought of either of these strategies. Together, we worked out a list that made sense. My own "highest priority" item (a compass) was relegated to last place on the list. One of the members said, "It should be thrown in the bushes."

As the group's "leader," I presented our results to the larger group. We graded our results and compared our team's list with our own original list and measured how much the list had changed. I won hands-down. My original list (now shown to be very stupid) had morphed into a pretty good list, thanks to my teammates. Unbeknownst to us, our group interactions had been observed through a one-way mirror, and as I was congratulated on my "prize," the observers were actually *laughing* as they left the booth.

"Don't go camping with her," one of them chuckled.

"Yeah, good leadership skills though," another conceded.

"That's *leadership*?" I thought, "That's just organization and group dynamics—that's easy!"

It seemed like faint praise at the time, but as the years have passed, I've come to appreciate the importance and value of being able to bring a team together to reach consensus and solve problems.

CEOs report they spend the majority of their time working on personnel issues. Hooray! This may be an area of strength for you, and you'll be one step ahead when you get to a senior executive level. Women are often very skilled at understanding people, being empathetic, and verbalizing difficult messages. They can be extraordinarily talented in dealing with personnel problems, and sometimes very adept at improving team dynamics. If you have strong skills in these areas, appreciate how much this will help you be a *great* leader.

Good Leaders Speak Up

I must sound like a broken record now since you've heard about the importance of speaking up throughout the book. It's even more important at the highest levels of the organization. Ask questions, show interest, stay actively involved in all the meetings you attend, and participate. If something doesn't make sense to you, question it. Don't be passive during a presentation. Your interest in the presenter's topic will translate into energy for him or her and stimulate the rest of the audience to get engaged.

You can demonstrate this leadership trait at all levels of the organization, as well as out in the world at large, at local community meetings, in the grocery store, in line at the ski lift. People who speak up make the world go round. This skill may come easily to you, or you may struggle to overcome your own humility and shyness. Remember both are blessings *and* curses. If you shoot your mouth off easily, you have to temper that natural inclination with softening preambles so you don't sound like a know-it-all and irritate people. On the other hand, if you have to force yourself to intervene when you would prefer to stay in the background, your general demeanor will show you're a humble person, and you are less likely to be criticized for acting like a big shot. No matter what your character is, you can enhance or soften certain traits in order to become more successful.

May You Not Be This Stupid...

Let's pause here for some counter-examples. Senior executives, especially CEOs, have notoriously short tenures, and some executives I worked with failed so fast it made my head spin. I've observed some keen reasons why. The guidance in this chapter isn't trivial, but some executives seemed determined to do just the opposite before they went down in flames.

In *two* places I worked, the first thing the new CEO did was bring in his spouse to spend copious amounts of money redecorating the executive suite. Unless your husband is an interior decorator, you're unlikely to make this incredibly bone-headed move, but please don't do anything similar. Particularly if you've been brought in because the company is in trouble, this type of move will be extremely unpopular with the employees.

Don't underestimate the stress that comes with these positions. These days, boards of directors seem to expect that a new CEO will turn a company around overnight, and the demanding phone calls and performance pressure start after a week on the job. One poor fellow I worked with was fired after six months and blamed for bad clinical results even though those trials had been underway for years. It was as though the board needed a scapegoat so they didn't have to admit what had happened on their watch. Unfortunately, I've observed first-hand how this pressure can handicap and wound a new chief executive.

Frequently, the immediate reaction is to isolate himself from his staff, partly because he doesn't want to tell them how crazy the board is, and partly because he doesn't want to confess that he's under attack. As you know from this chapter, that's exactly the *wrong* thing to do. Another reaction is to check out. Some of them just stop showing up to work. One guy I worked with went on *four* ski trips during the six months leading up to his dismissal. Sometimes I didn't even know he'd left until I went to look for him.

The following mistake is likely to be the last because it's the kiss of death: hiding bad news from the board. Again, sadly, I've observed that CEOs under attack, and worried about their jobs, begin to scrub the information that goes to the board. They start to live in a fantasy world where everything is fine; they are in denial about—or refuse to hear—any bad news. One poor soul I worked with wanted to meet with me to discuss alternate working hours for all employees the week before the company declared bankruptcy. That was one of the more surreal meetings of my career.

Good Leaders Are Ethical

Now we'll come full-circle and talk about that set of values you identified when you started out on this mission. We talked about being your own girl and that you would stay true to your core values through thick and thin, no matter what surprises or hazardous obstacles were thrown in your path. It's as important at the top of the organization as it has been throughout your rise. In honorable institutions, values, ethical behavior, and integrity start at the top and trickle down to all employees. As a leader, you embody those values, and your behavior must reinforce them. Think about how easy this is now. Because you established this moral core at the beginning, you're prepared to be the ethical leader your company needs. You're not in a scramble to figure out what you believe in and what kind of company you want to run. And your integrity—that you demonstrate now and have done throughout your career— allows you to hold your head high and bask in the confidence that you are a good and true leader and that your company will flourish with you at the helm.

CHAPTER ELEVEN
The Diamond

"A diamond is merely a lump of coal that did well under pressure."

I WANT YOU TO BELIEVE IN YOURSELF and assume that you can take on a challenge instead of focusing on how unprepared you are. Women's limitations at work often stem from a lack of self-confidence. That's understandable since you're in a man's world, but you're probably capable of more than you think. Somehow we seem to be wired to think more about what we don't have instead of what we do. We have to take risks to rise above our comfort zone and discover our potential. The more you practice behaviors that are hard for you, the easier they become. And what doesn't break you will make you stronger. That's how you become a diamond.

Here's an example very close to my heart. Remember how I always ask, "Did anyone die?" This is why.

After I'd reached a senior level, the head of human resources called me at home one night to tell me the body of one of the employees had been found. He had committed suicide—*at the office*. This man, who had previously reported to me, was a wonderful, gentle Swiss man, technically skilled, with a sly sense of humor. He was also gay. My heart broke when I heard he'd killed himself. The head of human resources told me she and the CEO had agreed I should address the employees the next day.

"I can't, I can't," I sobbed into the phone. "I'm too upset. I don't think I can do it."

But, within minutes, I realized I had to. I was a sensible choice because I knew him well. And the employees needed this. It was important. I *had* to do it.

Somehow that night, I found the words to use the next day to comfort them, remind them of Jean-Paul's modesty, how he wouldn't want them to be sad, some of the funny things he did, and how much he had loved working with them. As I watched their frozen shocked faces relax, saw even a few smiles, and felt the group draw a deep therapeutic breath, I thought, "I can do this."

And so can you. I hope you keep this book nearby for your entire career, and that its words inspire you to persevere to get what you want and comfort you when times are hard. I hope you read the "Whose Girl Are You?" and "Guiding Lights" sections if you're threatened or discouraged. I hope you read the chapter about Guys when you run across some oddball or another. Most of all, I hope you read this final chapter frequently. It's important, and look how short it is!

You're tougher than you think. You can do it. Shine on.

CPSIA information can be obtained at www.ICGtesting.com
Printed in the USA
LVOW131726281212

313626LV00004B/554/P